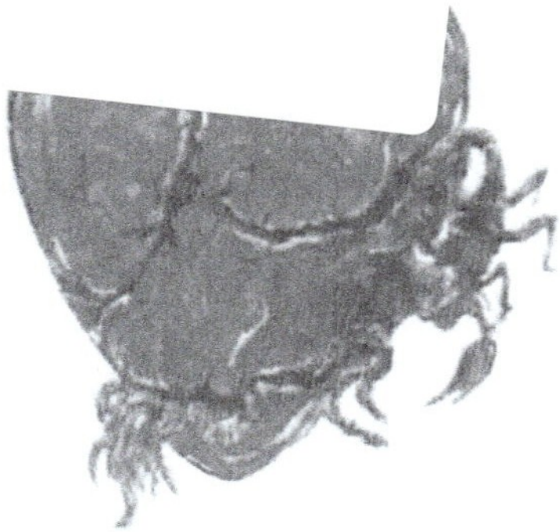

THE MADNESS OF THE HEART

MOUNTAIN OF FIRE AND MIRACLES MINISTRIES

Dr. D. K. OLUKOYA

THE MADNESS OF THE HEART

DR. D. K. OLUKOYA

THE MADNESS OF THE HEART

ISBN 978-36917-6-7
1st Printing - March, 2004AD

A Publication of
Mountain of Fire and Miracles Ministries
Press House
13, Olasimbo Street, off Olumo Road,
(By Unilag 2nd Gate), Onike, Iwaya,
P. O. Box 2990, Sabo, Yaba, Lagos, Nigeria.
website: www.mountain-of-fire.com
email: mfmhqworldwide@mountainoffire.org

All Scripture quotation is from the King James Version
Cover illustration: Sister Shade Olukoya

All rights reserved.
Reproduction in whole or part without written permission is prohibited.

TABLE OF CONTENTS

1 Idols of The Heart

To start off the topic of this chapter, let us examine Ezekiel 14:1-4:

Then came certain of the elders of Israel unto me, and sat before me. [2]And the word of the LORD came unto me, saying, [3]Son of man, these men have set up their idols in their heart, and put the stumbling block of their iniquity before their face; should I be enquired of at all by them? [4]Therefore speak unto them, and say unto them, Thus saith the Lord GOD; Every man of the house of Israel that setteth up his idols in his heart, and putteth the stumblingblock of his iniquity before his face, and cometh to the prophet; I the LORD will answer him that cometh according to the multitude of his idols;

And in verses 9 and 10, the Lord continues:

And if the prophet be deceived when he hath spoken a thing, I the LORD have deceived that prophet, and I will stretch out my hand upon him, and will destroy

him from the midst of my people Israel. [10]And they shall bear the punishment of their iniquity: the punishment of the prophet shall be even as the punishment of him that seeketh unto him;

The elders of the house of Israel had come to the man of God to inquire of the Lord. They wanted information from God. We would have thought that somebody that decided to see a prophet meant well. But before these people went to meet the prophet, they already had their own idols in their hearts. And because they had those idols in their hearts, the Lord said that the reply they would get would be according to these idols.

This means that if anyone has an idol inside him and goes to meet a prophet to seek information, the Lord would ask that prophet to answer him according to the idol in his heart.

If you have an idol, you will surely get the wrong information.

So, the Lord said, "If the prophet be deceived," because the person who came to meet the prophet had an idol in his heart.

Many people have idols hidden in the secret chambers of their hearts, hidden from the sight of men but definitely not from the sight of God. So, Hebrews 4:13 is an interesting verse:

Neither is there any creature that is not manifest in his sight: but all things are naked and opened unto the eyes of him with whom we have to do.

This means that as far as God is concerned, all the things that many people are trying to hide "are so naked before His eyes." That is, as far as these things are concerned, they are open before His eyes and He is seeing them quite clearly.

It may be painful to admit this, beloved, but it is true that a lot of people have idols in their hearts, and it is the idols that decide what they get most of the time they come to a prayer meeting. The only trouble is that the Christian idol is harder to recognise than that of the world.

While we were in the junior school in those days, we were taught a song that says, "Break down every idol in our hearts . . ." But I did not understand it. I wondered how a small boy like myself could have idols in my heart.

My picture of an idol was the carved head Ogun, (the god of iron) or other such things. However, as I matured, I began to understand what the Lord meant by "to break down every idol in our hearts."

The Bible says it is out of the abundance of the heart that the mouth speaks. This means that when the heart is full, it will pour out its content.

Have you ever met someone who has verbal diarrhoea? When such a person speaks, it does come from his heart. It is what a person has in his heart that comes out of his mouth.

There was a time we ran counselling for some people. Among them were a couple. I cannot now remember what the woman said that angered the husband to the extent that he called upon a local idol to break the head of the woman's father! This brought out an involuntary shout of "Christian!" from my mouth, whereupon the man began to apologise for his demonic utterance.

The truth is that the idea was first in the heart of the man before it came out of his mouth. He tried to hide for quite a while but the time definitely came when he was exposed.

The Bible says that everything is naked: all fornicators are naked, all adulterers are naked. So, before God, everything appears as on a television set.

There was a man who thought he was enjoying life. He got invited to a church but he never went, even though he said his father was a catechist.

One day, however, as he was sitting on his chair, somebody tapped him and said, "You have an appointment." Before he could say "Jesus is Lord," the person just pulled out his spirit from his body just like pulling clothes out of somebody's body. He began, too, to ask questions: "Where are we going?"

The angel asked him to be patient: "You'll soon know." Eventually, he landed before the throne of God. He could not behold the glory and the light there. He bowed down and God sounded out his name and said to him, "You are 25 years behind the schedule I have for you," adding that before He would start the work with him, it was necessary to do a review of his life.

And suddenly, there came something like a television screen on which the man's life began to show right from the time his mother gave birth to him to the moment of his presence before the Lord. All the sinful things he had done - abortion for his girlfriends, encouraging people to sin against God, all forms of fornication -all played back before his naked eyes.

When he watched the playback up to a point, he asked God to turn the television off. God told him that it was unnecessary to continue as each scene represented a page in the book of his life. He asked God to send him back so that he would have the chance to make amendments. He said he was a scientist while on earth hence he didn't believe many things that were told him about God. God replied that He was a scientist too.

At any rate, He was kind enough to return him to earth. When he got back, he became a devoted Christian. While this man was able to get a second chance, others like him may not be so lucky. Their idols pull them in eternal perdition.

Any person, thing, attitude, endeavour, concept, doctrine or object that can replace God in your life is an idol. Anything you place before God or by the side of God is an idol in your life. A lot of Christians have secret idols in their lives. It is these secret idols that get us into trouble.

When some people come to see a prophet or a man of God, they may not necessarily get a message from God. God is mute in most instances because the person who has approached His servant for solution to his problem has an idol in his heart.

If you are a very good reader of the Bible you must have discovered that one of the men that the Bible condemns so much is Jeroboam.

Whoever committed iniquity in the Bible, the Bible would say, "And he committed iniquity like Jeroboam." And what did Jeroboam do? He set up one idol in Dan and another one in Bethel and called the people of Israel together and said, "You house of Israel, behold the god that delivered you from the land of Egypt." And God didn't take it lightly at all.

But before Jeroboam set up the physical idols on the ground, they had started in his heart. Something happened: Jeroboam's son fell seriously sick, and because Jeroboam was far from God, he did not even know that the prophet of God in Israel called Ahijah was already blind. So when he asked for the baby to be taken to the prophet so that he could say whether or not it would live, he told his wife to disguise so that the prophet would not recognise her. The woman dressed like a man.

At any rate, as she got to the door and knocked, a voice came from inside: "Come thou in, you wife of Jeroboam! Why feigneth thyself to be another?" And before she could talk, the man of God already knew why she came. "Is it not to know whether or not your sick son will live? And thus saith the Lord, He shall die!" Why? Because there was an idol in Jeroboam's life.

Some people come to the Mountain of Fire and Miracles Ministries and when they have stayed a while and found that our mode of worship does not accommodate their sinful ways, they run away. What pushes them out is one thing, the idol in their lives. When God puts you in a position and asks you to serve Him there but you keep giving conditions, that thing which makes you to give conditions is an idol in your life.

God asked Saul, "Hath the Lord greater delight in burnt sacrifices and offerings than hearkening to His voice?" He said, "Behold, obedience is better than sacrifice and to hearken than the fat of rams."

And He added that "stubbornness is like iniquity and

idolatry, and rebellion is like witchcraft. So a witch and a rebellious person are twins bound for hell fire. A stubborn person and an idol worshipper are twins in hell fire.

MODERN-DAY IDOLS

These days we have a lot of modern-day idols that people worship and these are cleverly hidden.

Wealth/Money

A lot of people spend their whole lifetime running after money and the only language they understand is money. When asked to pray, they excuse themselves by saying they will get serious with the Lord after they have made their first millions naira. Even when they absent themselves from prayer meeting, they always give as an excuse their drive to make ends meet.

I know a man who spent as much as x30,000:00 to treat a boil in his neck, whereas his monthly salary is not more than x3,500. This shows that only Jesus really makes ends meet for us.

"Seek ye first the kingdom of God and all other things (like wealth, etc.) shall be added unto you." But when you seek other things first, you have an idol in your heart.

The Bible says, "I have been young, but now I am old, I have not yet seen the righteous being forsaken or his children begging bread."

There is no man who sought the kingdom of God first and its righteousness and ever remained poor.

Think of it: What is the use of all the money a person has gathered all of his lifetime only for him to end up in hell fire?

Or what is the use of the money a man has spent his whole lifetime gathering when those coming behind him are impatiently waiting for him to die so that they could take it over?

And in this worshipping of wealth, the church is not left out. As churches grew, we find that what a man does in order to make money does not matter anymore. All such churches do invite people to come so that they can obtain prosperity and give part of it to the church.

Fame

Another modern-day idol is fame. Many people forget that even if the whole world knows a man and God does not know him such a fellow is wasting his time and efforts.

Present World Pleasure

Another idol in the present world is pleasure. A lot of people simply want to relax and enjoy even when the evil one schemes to tear their lives apart.

Knowledge

A lot of people have turned their certificates to their gods. The search for knowledge has replaced God in their lives.

Power

God hates idolatry with perfect hatred. That is why His first commandment is: "Ye shall have no other god beside me." In other words, DON'T WORSHIP IDOLS! Once you ascribe what is due to God to an object, special demons move in and turn that thing into something that has power.

INTERNAL IDOLS

Internal idols would invite wicked spirits from outside, and until these internal idols are destroyed in the life of the Christian and thrown out, many evil things will remain in his life. Let us look at some of these idols.

Secret Hidden Idols

Many Christians move about with these. They would do themselves a world of good to look deep into their spirits as the enemy is looking at these things and using them as points of harassment.

God wants them to get rid of those idols so that when we come before His prophets He would use them to prosper us. But when there is an idol in your life, God will answer you according to that idol.

Unforgiveness

One idol that is very common in the lives of people is unforgiveness. If you live in a house where nobody agrees with you, you must have an idol in your life. The only valid reason the Bible allows for you where people don't agree with you is your faith. But where people don't agree with you because of some other things it means you have an idol.

You may paint this with any colour but an idol is an idol. It must be pulled down. Remember Him before whom all things are naked. Some Christians once lived together in a building. Because of the idol in their hearts, each would sweep the little area around his apartment ignoring that all of them shared a common passage.

Likewise some people can't forgive their pastors or their group leaders. But as long as this idol of unforgiveness remains in their hearts, the enemy will continue to point it out against them each time they approach God for assistance.

For instance, a woman once requested for prayer. Her life had been stable and prosperous but, suddenly, things fell apart for her. Even the foreign countries she had been visiting in the past without any problem now began to refuse her entry. Her three vehicles had run aground and she could hardly make ends meet. Then she ran to me for prayer.

But just as I was about to start praying with her, the Lord told me: "Son, there's somebody this woman cannot forgive."

I stopped the prayer and turned to the woman and told her what God had just told me and asked her to go first to forgive that person. She looked at me and said, "I know, it's my husband." I asked her why it was very difficult for her to forgive him and she replied that it was just impossible for her to do so.

She recounted her husband's rise from grass to grace and what role she played then, only to be swept aside for a 16-year old girl whom he brought in as his new wife. "Not only that," she continued, "He drove me out of his mansion and restricted me to the boys' quarters! How can you forgive such a man? How?"

I told her that the Bible says she must still forgive that man. She was unimpressed and not only stormed out in anger, but also forgot her bag in my office.

All this notwithstanding, the woman was the first person to get to church the following day. She smiled at me and after the prayer meeting she came to me and told me that she was ready to forgive. We prayed and the woman asked God to forgive her unforgiveness.

Right from the following day, and within a week, all the blessings she had been blocking with her unforgiving spirit for over five years totally fell into place. That unforgiving spirit was the idol in her heart and for as long as it remained there, God held back His own blessings.

Bitterness

For some people, their own idol is bitterness. They

endlessly hold on to the wrong done by someone somewhere, and for as long as they hold on to this, the enemy uses it against them.

Jealousy

Jealousy is the idol a lot more people have in their lives. They easily grow envious of other people's achievements and progress. For as long as such people cannot be happy seeing the good in the lives of others, nothing good ever happens to them.

There is no way a person can harbour these three idols of unforgiveness, bitterness and jealousy without nursing hatred. Any believer that nurses hatred is a sure candidate for hell fire. This has to be well understood.

Discouragement

Another secret idol in the hearts of many Christians is discouragement. Many Christians get easily discouraged. They tend to backslide or give up efforts at turning things around in their lives. They make some attempts and expect to see a miracle overnight. But when this does not happen as they expect, they become discouraged and even begin to doubt God.

I once shared the vision of one sister who cried herself to sleep. Her fiancé had suddenly warned her to keep off his house and she thought she should end her life.

During her sleep she saw the vision of herself walking up and down a very big market. She eventually got to a particular stall where the devil was selling things. All she could see on display at this satanic stall was hypertension, diabetes, bad luck- all with price tags. Then the sister asked the devil which of these items carried the highest price tag.

The devil replied, "discouragement," adding that once he got believers discouraged and they were unhappy, he easily captured them. "After they've been so effectively captured," he went on, "I then add depression, but that one comes free of charge." Of course, discouragement and depression combine to give birth to a child of their own which is hopelessness.

Worry

Yet another idol that has found a comfortable home in the hearts of many Christians is worry. This makes a great many people look older than their actual age. They easily get upset by life's troubling circumstances.

Confusion

In the lives of others, it is confusion. And when you put worry and confusion together in the same place they give birth to their own offspring, fear. This, too, is present in many lives and it is an idol that must be cast out.

Impatience

Impatience is another terrible idol that has made the lives of many Christians miserable. Patience is a virtue. Even those who seldom read the Bible can acknowledge that "patience can cook stone." Indeed, patience is one of the greatest virtues that God has given to man. The patient person always laughs last, whereas the impatient man would with his own hand upset the table the Lord has graciously set before him.

It is said that the perfect husband or the perfect wife is the one that agrees that he or she has married an imperfect partner. This makes the spouse not to look for any magic in the partner and to be content with whatever comes out of the union.

Selfishness

Another idol in the lives of so many Christians is selfishness. Whenever a prayer point is called in the church for our neighbours, the general reaction is for believers to wonder why their neighbours should take precedence when they have their own needs.

Hot Temper

Hot temper is another hidden idol believers have to deal with in their lives. When this combines with other aforementioned idols like impatience and selfishness a new offspring is generated, and that is demonic violence.

Filthy Thoughts

The minds of many Christians are filled up with filthy thoughts that constitute an idol in their lives. These are in the forms of evil imaginations, flirting, immorality, seduction and such other things that the believer should not be thinking of and which debar so many believers from receiving their miracles.

Of course, unless you are gifted, there is no way you can tell from the face of the believer whose heart is clean. These filthy thoughts are hidden far deep in the heart. They may not worship these idols outside but they are busy day and night worshipping them inside.

Doubt

Another idol in the minds of many believers is doubt. Many believers are clever doubters. When I was growing up as a Christian, if a person approached me for spiritual assistance, I usually gave it to him raw, I told him his problem the way I saw it. This made me to have a lot of enemies.

In one particular instance, I frankly told a sister who brought her domestic crisis to me that the person behind her problem was, indeed, her mother. The old woman had caged the sister. The sister couldn't believe this. She wondered what she could do and I told her all she had to do was serious prayer. She did not know how to pray and asked me to teach her. The following day, the first person I saw at my door was this sister and her mother.

As I came out to meet them, the old woman turned to her daughter, and asked, "Is this the pastor that said I am a witch?" Seeing the rage in the eyes of the old woman, I began to scheme how to extricate myself from the web of crisis staring me in the face. I have since known better. These days, all I do is to give people prayers to pray on their own so that God can open their eyes to see the truth about their situations.

There was this other sister for whom things had turned upside down. She ran to me for assistance. As she stepped into the church, the invisible woman behind her problem followed her in. She couldn't see her but I did. On the forehead of the invisible woman was the inscription: MOTHER. Quite conscious of all the problems I had run into in the past, I had to find a way of telling the truth without getting into any trouble once again.

I found a way round the matter by telling the sister that the person behind her problem was someone she was always buying things for. The sister said there were so many people she was buying things for. Then I mentioned there was a particular favoured one among the lot.

To help her further I gave her some prayer points that would enable her to: (1) identify all her hidden enemies, (2) identify the doors through which they were entering her life and (3) realise all the harms which they had done in her life.

The sister eyed me disdainfully and wanted to book another appointment with me. When I replied that, that was all I had for her, she hissed and walked away throwing the prayer points on the floor.

The next time I heard of her, she was already in a psychiatric hospital - stark mad. However, once in a fleeting moment in that state of madness, she remembered the prayer points I gave her. She was helped by the Holy Spirit to start praying them until she began to see exactly the same thing I·had told her but she could not believe. She saw her mother eating live snakes. Immediately the vision cleared away, the person the woman saw was her mother. She came to greet her in the hospital. It was then the daughter knew what to do.

When a person cages another person's destiny and the caged person still goes to take breakfast from the table of his captor, all that he is doing is strengthening the bondage every day.

Doubt is a demon that constitutes an idol in the lives of many people, and the Bible says that "a doubting man is like the waves of the sea . . . tossed here and there, and that such a person should not hope to get anything from the Lord."

Some people have a high level of doubt that often makes them ask if there is such a being called God.

Indecision

Indecision is another idol that has distressed so many people.

Pride

Pride is yet another. It fills people with self-exaltation and unteachable spirit.

All these, like the other idols, create other smaller hidden idols.

With this state of affairs, it means that many people have traders in the temple of their lives who are busy buying and selling. These traders must be chased out by the Lion of Judah.

SOLUTIONS

The problem with idols is that they shut God's face away. God would not take a look wherever they exist. This is why problems persist in the lives of many Christians, to the extent that they begin to wonder if God exists.

The truth is that no matter what they go through, as long as idols remain in their lives, God would keep His distance from them.

I have once shared and would share again the story of a medical doctor who died and his wife prayed for his soul to return to life. As the woman prayed for a long while, the husband miraculously came back to life.

However, while the man remained dead, he saw himself arriving where somebody held him by the right arm and another held him by the left arm and they dragged him along. His first thought was that they were taking him to heaven but as they dragged him along, he began to feel heat. It was at that point that he remembered the Bible. It occurred to him that if he was really bound for heaven there shouldn't be so much heat.

He started begging his arresters to leave him alone and they simply ignored him until they dragged him to hell. According to his testimony, it was at the borderline into hell fire that he saw people being dumped into hell fire like tipper lorry dumping sand into one big valley. He was amazed, but just as he was about to be tossed into hell fire, a voice came from heaven asking that he be released. Immediately he was released, the devil came out to tell God that He had no right to take the medical doctor to heaven, just for one reason, the adultery that was in his heart. The devil said that the man might be acquitted of all other iniquities but there was no way he could be exonerated from this singular sin.

If the devil could hold one single sin against the medical doctor, we can imagine what he would do against many believers with as many as four or five sins.

God had no other option than to agree with the devil on this point. He couldn't be lying to God anyway since he knows the truth about each of us.

All the same, while agreeing that the medical doctor did not qualify for heaven, the Lord said He would not put him in hell. Because He had seen his wife praying, the Lord said He would return him to life to enable him to correct his ways.

The man had been a devoted Christian and a very good Sunday school teacher, but while he maintained these fine credentials he had that idol of adultery in his heart which paved his way to hell.

You either deal with the idol in your heart or you allow it to deal with you.

PRAYER POINTS

1. O Lord, show me the hidden idols in my life, in the name of Jesus.

2. O Lord, deliver me from secret idols, in the name of Jesus.

3. (Lay your hand on your chest) O Lord, break down every idol in my life, in the name of Jesus.

4. I cast out every idol from my heart, in the name of Jesus.

5. Every family idol, I break you down and cast you out, in the name of Jesus.

6. Every inherited idol of the heart, I break you down and cast you out, in the name of Jesus.

7. Every idol of marriage destruction, I break you down and cast you out, in the name of Jesus.

8. Every stubborn idol of the heart, I break you down and cast you out, in the name of Jesus.

9. Every idol of confusion, I break you down and cast you out, in the name of Jesus.

10. Let the fire of God boil all rivers harbouring my enemies, in the name of Jesus.

11. Let the blood of Jesus wipe out all my evil dreams, in the name of Jesus.

12. I command all my good dreams to come to pass, in the name of Jesus.

13. I destroy every satanic accident organised for my sake, in the name of Jesus.

2 The Madness of The Heart

DIAGNOSIS OF THE MIND

The Bible contains the best diagnosis as well as the best medication for achieving a wholesome mind. Those who are sick cannot achieve good health unless proper diagnosis of the sickness is carried out and proper medication is applied.

The human mind can be mad without any prominent sign of a visible ailment. Many whose minds or hearts are mad look like perfect gentlemen in the public.

The greatest form of insanity is that which can be found in the mind. It is easy to detect or identify a madman in the street, but it is very difficult to detect secret madness of the heart. The truth is that the secret madness of the mind is as serious as the physical madness which makes the patient to eat from garbage heaps.

The Bible has identified what is regarded as the madness of the mind. This shocking revelation is given to us in the book of Ecclesiastes 9:3:

This is an evil among all things that are done under the sun, that there is one event unto all, yea, also the heart of the sons of men is full of evil, and madness is in their heart while they live, and after that they go to the dead.

There is a strong link between the mind and the conscience. The conscience is a reflection of what is on the human mind. A good heart will always produce a wholesome conscience. That is why the Bible warns: "Keep thy heart with all diligence; for out of it are the issues of life" (Prov.4:23). Here, the Bible enjoins every believer to protect the mind from all evil influences.

Why is the heart so important that it occupies a central place in the lives of all men and women?

The mind is the only link which we have with God. We are made alive unto God through our minds. We perceive the truth of the Scriptures with our hearts and we make all our efforts towards worshipping God through the human mind. That is why the Bible commands:

And thou shalt love the Lord thy God with all thy heart, and with all thy soul, and with all thy mind and with all thy strength: this is the first commandment (Mark 12:30).

It is important to keep the mind in good condition. If anything goes wrong with it, the whole of your life will be turned upside down.

A lot of people wonder why most of the words which men speak in the society today are evil. We do not need to go too far to understand the reason. The Bible makes it very clear that the heart of man is full of evil and that madness resides in the hearts of men and women. Many people cannot control the words they speak because of the madness of the mind. We need to understand what the madness of the mind is all about.

There are various levels of madness. There is hyper-madness and there is mild-madness.

What comes to your mind when you see a male prophet bathing a lady by the side of the river? That is an example of madness.

Somebody loses his temper and rages violently. That is another example of madness. Something is wrong with the mind or the conscience.

A lot of things are happening today. I had an experience when I was in the secondary school, several years ago. There was a preacher who came to the bus-stop early in the morning to preach to a little crowd trying to enter vehicles. I never saw a single person who waited behind to listen to the preacher who appeared not to be in total control of his mind.

I had a very troublesome classmate who decided to tell the elderly man to think of a better way of preaching the gospel: "Papa, you appear to have been wasting your time. Why do you stand at this bus-stop preaching when nobody is listening to you? Why don't you preach to them when they are through with their daily duties? Or why don't you go to a place where you can find people who are ready to listen to you?"

The elderly man said, "Thank you, my son. That is very thoughtful of you. Let me help you by giving you some passages in Psalms. Use the passages for your exams and you will always come out in flying colours."

We were surprised, to find the same preacher at the same bus-stop the following day preaching to the same people who were so much in a hurry that they found it difficult to spare one minute. The man had a problem which bordered on the madness of the mind.

There are many mad people in the streets today. They are well-dressed, intelligent and appear normal, but they are mentally sick.

There is partial madness and there is complete madness. When somebody runs mad (whether it is partial or total) it means that he has lost control of his mind. That is exactly what happens to those who are drunk. They lose every sense of decency.

Let us look at the characteristics of madness of the mind.

The mind is the greatest battle field. If your mind is already captured there is no battle, you can fight and win. A lot of people who go from one hospital to another would be healed if they can pray about the healing of the mind. Many people do not know that their problems can be traced to the mind.

The best thing to do, therefore, is to know how to deal with the problem of the mind.

There will be less problems and sicknesses in the society if the problems of the mind are properly dealt with.

THE SYMPTOMS OF MADNESS OF THE MIND

What then are the symptoms of the madness of the mind?

Worry

It is spiritual madness for anyone to sit down and sing about God's sufficient grace one moment and to lament his problems of life next moment. The contradiction which is expressed shows that such a person is suffering from the madness of the mind. He must address this serious issue.

If you have this kind of problem, you must deal with it seriously. Failure to do so may lead you into more serious problems. Your mind may become a battle zone. You might even go into total backsliding from that stage.

Worry and anxiety are among our greatest problems today. I get close to 1,000 letters a week from those who believe that their matters require urgent attention. I have discovered that a good number of them only need someone to talk with.

If you allow the devil to reduce you to a worry bag he will introduce several other problems into your life.

Feeling that one is completely useless

Some people write themselves off completely by concluding that they are good for nothing or useless. Such people go about complaining: "What kind of life is this? Everything is upside down. Maybe, I should end it all."

After making such a statement, the devil would give them several suggestions. He may tell them: "You can jump down from a very high bridge or hang yourself with a rope. You can drink poison. That would be a very quick way of ending everything." If you feel that your life is totally useless or that you are tired of life, this is satan at work.

Depression

Depression is one of the most terrible problems that can plague the human heart. The Bible calls it the spirit of Heaviness. There is a heavy load on the minds of those who are going through moments of depression.

Some people become so depressed that they do not want to talk to anybody. There are others who become so depressed that they lock themselves up in a room for several days.

I know a man who experienced such an attack. He came back to Nigeria from England after obtaining a degree. He got a good job and was full of great expectations. Having studied in England, he expected things to go on perfectly. But things became worse because he was also a stickler for perfection, punctuality and excellence. He was employed as a manager in a company and hardly had he started the job than the entire company turned upside down.

The official resumption time was 7.30 a.m and if anyone resumed after 7.30 a.m. he was disciplined. He gave lots of queries to members of staff for coming late to the office. The people who were given queries began to deal with him. Things became so bad that the chairman of the company had to query him: "Manager, what is this company being turned into? We've been running the company before you came. Why don't you take it easy? This is not England. This is Nigeria."

The man refused to listen to the chairman and was eventually given a letter of termination of appointment. He couldn't get another job for a very long time and He became so depressed that he decided to lock himself up and refused to talk to anyone. He went into what can be called the madness of the mind.

High-mindedness

A lot of people are so high-minded that they live in the world of fantasy. They mind high things and esteem themselves above measure.

Some people go about saying, "I'm going to ride in the latest brand of Mercedes Benz for my wedding." That is a typical example of high-mindedness. What impact will the latest brand of Mercedes have on your marriage? Some people would say, "The state governor will be the chairman of my wedding reception." That is how far high-mindedness can take its victims.

High-mindedness will lead you into unreasonable actions. It will convert you into a victim of the madness of the mind. It will corrupt your conscience.

Sadness

There is a kind of sadness that is not ordinary. Some people become sad for no just reason. They are sad before they go to bed at night and they wake up early in the morning, feeling terribly sad. It is an evidence that the mind is mad.

Hopelessness

Many people feel that their situation is completely hopeless. This is another symptom of madness of the mind.

Guilt

A lot of people feel guilty for what does not really exist. If you committed a sin 15 years ago, God has forgiven you. Instead of accepting God's forgiveness, you go about harassing yourself over what God no longer remember. How long will you allow guilt to keep haunting you?

The guilt, which many people are going through today does not emanate from the devil, the accuser of the brethren. It is self-made. The guilt, which you have allowed to hang on your mind like a dark cloud, emanates from your own heart, not from the devil.

Dwelling in the past

Those who dwell in the past experience madness of the mind. Some people spend their lives living in the distant past. Why must you worry about yesterday? Yesterday is gone forever. You must not worry about previous situations and problems since you cannot go back to them.

Inability to concentrate

A lot of people cannot control their minds. They cannot focus their hearts on a single subject or matter. They vacillate over several matters and situations without being able to lay hold on anyone. Something is wrong with their minds.

Lack of confidence

This is a symptom of madness of the mind. People who fall into lack of self -confidence, feel timid and are not able to face anything without feeling inferior.

Anger

This is another evidence of madness of the mind. A lot of people erupt into violent anger when there is no reason to do so.

Fear of death

Many people spend all their lives thinking of death. That is a symptom of madness of the mind.

Lack of motivation

This category of people face life situations without any iota of interest or excitement.

Addiction to weeping

There are people who are easily moved to tears whenever there is a little problem. They live as if they are addicted to crying. That is another instance of the madness of the mind.

Feeling of isolation

Talk to some people and they would give you the impression that everyone on earth is against them. That is a clear example of the sickness of the mind. Why must you allow that kind of feeling to bother you? Even if everyone on earth was against you, the fact that God is on your side makes you an overcomer.

Vagabond

The human mind is the greatest vagabond in the universe. You might be in a particular place while your mind has travelled thousands of miles away. If you refuse to put that kind of vagabond condition of the mind under control, it will eventually lead you into serious problems.

It is unfortunate that what psychiatric hospitals are doing is to collect house rents when the rooms of people's lives are already hired out. Some people's minds have also been converted to concrete slabs by the devil. They cannot make any progress in life.

Abode of evil cobwebs

Many minds are also abodes of evil cobwebs. Such people are fond of running away from God whenever God is trying to reach out to them. The only thing that can bring progress into their lives is change. Unfortunately, many hate change. They want things to continue the same way. Many people who claim that they have open minds are only deceiving themselves. Their minds are closed.

There is no free thinker anywhere. Jesus called a spade a spade during His earthly ministry. He denounced all the evil things which people do. He is the only preacher who talked most about hell fire. Although He came to demonstrate love, He spoke the truth.

There is nothing like a liberal mind. God gives us no room for such. If you go about saying that you have a liberal mind you are living in a self-deceit.

Somebody was called a brother and he flared up. He was angry because the other fellow referred to him as a brother. He said, "Me, a brother? How can you call me brother so and so? Don't you know that I am a man of God? Don't call me brother so and so. Call me pastor or reverend so and so. I won't allow you to put me in the same category with ordinary Christians. Don't ever make that mistake again."

But why should someone get angry because he was called a brother? That was an evidence of possessing a mean mind. Mean minds react to little things while great minds respond to great things.

Anyone who constantly thinks of himself will end up becoming discouraged. If you centre all your thoughts on yourself you will easily get tired of yourself.

Again, I want you to know that it takes a strong mind to control a wild tongue. If your mind is loose, your tongue will also run loose. If your heart is open to satanic incursion it will soon become a dustbin for all kinds of garbage.

It is very dangerous to invite enemies into your mind. The devil would give you topics to deliberate upon.

If you go to a proper school of deliverance, one of the first lessons they would teach you is that every demon has its own assignment. You will also discover that every geographical area is controlled by a territorial spirit or a ruling demon. You will also discover that there is a Yoruba demon, an Hausa demon, an Igbo demon, an Urhobo demon and a Swahili demon. They would also teach you that there is something called a strongman who is in charge of junior demons in the evil world.

One thing which they will also teach you is that the demon of anger is the gate-keeper over the lives of men and women.

The demon of anger stands at the gate as an executive gateman. The moment you get angry, he would open the gate and beckon to his other colleagues telling them that time is right for them to come in and take control. Problems like diseases, hypertension, poverty and demonic attacks will quickly rush in. By the time your anger subsides they would have succeeded in taking total control of your life. That is how problems would take residence in your life waiting for another time of momentary madness.

A sister dragged her husband to me saying: "This is the foolish man. It's because of him I have tried to book this appointment." The man said, "Man of God, I am really sorry to disturb you. I decided to follow her to your office because I know that she can kill me if I did not. However, I must tell you that I am grateful to God that actually if not because of this church, it could have been worse than this. I've continued to encourage her to keep on coming to your church because I've detected slight changes in her life."

That was what anger did in the life of that sister. I hope that does not describe your own situation. If you are in the same shoes with her, you need deliverance as well as complete overhauling of your life.

A lot of people will go to hell fire if their lives are not totally free from evil influences. If you are only partially free, your heart is the devil's property. That is why the Bible challenges every believer to renew his or her mind through the word of God.

When you get born again, you need the word of God to wipe off every old debris of your former life. As you continue to renew your mind through the word of God, you will begin to experience wonderful changes in your life.

You must ensure that the totality of your life is not the property of the devil. It becomes clear, therefore, that if you win a person's mind you have captured him. If you capture his thoughts you can control him. This explains why satan fights to capture the hearts of men and women. He knows that once he takes control of their hearts he has won the battle. The Bible says:

But I fear, lest by any means, as the serpent beguiled Eve through his subtilty, so your minds should be corrupted from the simplicity that is in Christ (2 Cor.11:3)

The devil is after the human mind. His goal is to corrupt the simplicity of your mind. He came to Eve in the Garden of Eden and manipulated her mind until she was influenced to disobey God.

Satan fed Eve's mind with lots of negative information until she decided to disobey God. She doubted the word of God and believed the lies of the devil. Her mind was corrupted from the simplicity which resided in it before the time of the fall.

What happened to Eve has happened to several other people today. More and more people are having their minds corrupted and shifted away from the simplicity of the gospel.

The moment that happens, the devil has succeeded in removing your feet from the solid rock. To stand on slippery ground is to fall.

I want you to lay your hand on your chest and take this prayer point: "My mind, go back to your resting place, in the name of Jesus."

There is no doubt that you know the state of your own heart. How do you think the Lord looks at your heart at this moment? If Jesus were to come to you right now and flash the torch of His holy and high standard towards your heart, what will His verdict be?

It is possible to appear respectable and godly outwardly and be filled with wickedness internally. You may look so holy outwardly as if you cannot even hurt a fly while your heart is filled with destruction, adultery, anger, worry and depression.

SATANIC SUGGESTIONS

One thing which the devil has continued to use with great success against the minds of people is suggestions. Suggestions are generally subtle. They look very attractive when viewed ordinarily. However, most suggestions are evil. If you do not know how to counter suggestions, you will find yourself agreeing with them. You will go out of your way to do what you did not intend to do.

When evil suggestions have completely taken over your heart, you will find yourself acting in the direction of those suggestions.

For example, the devil might tell you, "Don't you know how intelligent you are? Why should someone with your own kind of brain suffer poverty? Why don't you get smart and cheat your company? You could make millions of naira that way. After all, everybody is doing it."

The devil might also tell you, "Don't you know that you are very handsome. Handsome people like you are sure of getting married to the lady of your dream."

If you are a lady, The devil might also tell you, "What are you doing with your beauty? Why do you go about complaining that you have no money? Men will give you money, if you agree to go out with them."

All these are satanic suggestions. The devil is fond of giving smart suggestions. If somebody gives you an amount of money, the devil will be on hand to offer a suggestion saying, "Why don't you remove some amount of money and go back to the person and tell him that the money given to you was not complete? Talk to him as if you really mean what you are saying. If you do that you will make some money."

All these suggestions may lead you into all kinds of devilish practices if you listen to them.

Somebody entered a bus and found some money on the seat. He quickly grabbed it and felt like asking the commuters in the bus: "Who is the owner of this money?" The devil gave him a suggestion, "If you make such an announcement, you will lose the money. A smart fellow will claim that he or she is the owner." He accepted the satanic suggestion and went home joyfully with the money. He decided to kill his conscience by paying a tithe not knowing that he was paying a demonic tithe. That is how many people pay demonic tithes after acquiring wealth with their satanic methods.

The lists of satanic suggestions are endless. The devil generally tries to influence you to do what he knows is against the will of God. He has one strange pattern of behaviour: Generally going into a kind of evil laughter as soon as he has succeeded in achieving his goal, then he goes away leaving the person to struggle with the consequences of the violation of the word of God.

THE CONSCIENCE AND DEMONIC MANIPULATIONS

Why are people finding it easier to accept satanic suggestions? Why do they find it difficult to remember the Scriptures they have memorised?

Why do the minds of people wander about during prayer? Why do people, who are given wonderful revelations by God, wake up in the morning only to forget all these revelations?

These things take place because the conscience of most people is subjected to demonic manipulations.

The conscience can be likened to a theatre where all forms of satanic operations take place. The extent to which you allow the devil to influence your thought is the extent to which he can control you. The devil will continue to control you as long as you continue to give him free hand. You may say that you are speaking in tongues and that you are a spirit-filled Christian. All that will mean nothing to the devil as long as he continues to exercise dominion over your mind.

The conscience is the devil's target. Without access to the conscience, he will not be able to do anything. People's problems originate from the conscience. All these show us that the conscience is the centre of serious warfare.

The devil has instant and easy access to the consciences of most people. Nothing is hidden from the devil. He has a complete picture of your conscience, your thoughts, and your imaginations. Your motives, your intentions as well as your secret ambitions are all known to him. He is thoroughly familiar with your weaknesses and strengths.

The devil knows us more than most of us know ourselves. We often forget our past mistakes and overlook our weaknesses and strengths. If you permit him to work on your conscience, he would go ahead to plant evil ideas there.

He (the devil) stores every information which he ever finds in our hearts and uses them to give us suggestions regarding what he wants us to do.

Once the devil knows that something is your weakness, he goes ahead to use it against you. If he knows that you are easily moved to tears, he would bring situations that will make you to cry. He knows that once you cry you will be discouraged and the moment you are discouraged you will not be able to pray. He would programme such situations into your life until you are completely powerless. Then he would attack you.

You have to fight hard against all satanic suggestions. Once the devil tries a weapon against you, he will not leave you. He would expect you to be completely swept off your feet. If he knows that you are a worry bag he would constantly bring around you those things that will make you to worry. But if you say no to his suggestions, his weapons will become ineffective in your life.

The devil has continued to use different methods against human beings. He has continued to design evil suggestions in such a clever manner to make them match the weaknesses of people. He is not foolish, he does not give any suggestion that does not agree with your own feelings or desires. He generally gathers problems and places them on the platform of your background and peculiarity.

When these suggestions come they appear reasonable. The devil would make you to cooperate with unbelievers, join your business with them and make them your confidants. The alliance may appear beneficial on the surface. You may even go about, thinking that you are surrounded by good people. While this is going on, powers of darkness would be having a good laugh at you.

A sister went to a man of God and said, "Please, pray for me, I want to get married." The man of God decided to help the sister. He went to a mountain where he prayed for seven days to find out God's mind concerning her marriage. He came down with divine instructions for her. The man of God told her that God said she should marry a man who happened to be one-eyed.

She found it difficult to accept the man and made up her mind to disobey God and look for another man to present to her friends and colleagues. She actually succeeded and got married to a handsome man, but five years later, she lost her husband. The devil won. She lost.

The devil is an expert in offering suggestions that appear good and beneficial. He gives suggestions which are aimed at leading men and women into deception. Once he succeeds in manipulating the mind, physical and spiritual problems will follow. His success will also lead to man's failure, defeat, poverty, family breakdown, oppression, suicide, chronic sickness, profitless hard-work and other forms of attacks. The devil would bring terrible problems and attacks into the lives of victims because their minds have been captured.

Your life is determined by the state of your conscience. The conscience is the gateway to the spirit, soul and body. Your thought will determine your actions and your actions will determine your destiny.

Once again, I want you to close your eyes and take this prayer point: "Oh Lord, shine your divine light into my mind and let all strangers flee." The mind of man consists of two departments. There is the conscious mind and the subconscious mind. The conscious mind is the smallest compartment in the human mind. On the other hand, the subconscious mind is what you make use of for what happens to you on the spot.

The sub-conscious mind is made up of memories that are long as well as a summary of all that has happened to you since you were born. Children's experiences are stored in the mind. Traumatic experiences and other experiences that are embedded in the hearts of men are also stored up in the mind. When the sub-conscious mind becomes filled to the brim, the mind would begin to run mad. Once that kind of brimful experience comes into contact with daily experiences that border on stubborn problems the mind will become totally insane.

You accept forgiveness of sin in your conscious mind. Since the sub-conscious mind forms the greater part of the human mind, it has more impact upon our lives. Therefore, the subconscious mind must be renewed, changed, programmed and transformed by the word of God. The sub-conscious mind must be conformed to Christ if you want the totality of your heart to be wholesome. Failure to do this is to put your life under evil control.

Your mind must become the mind of Christ if you must experience total conformity to the character of Jesus Christ. You must not give yourself any rest until the totality of what is stated in Philipians 4:8 is fulfilled in your life:

Finally, brethren, whatsoever things are true, whatsoever things are honest, whatsoever things are just, whatsoever things are pure, whatsoever things are lovely, whatsoever things are of good report; if there be any virtue, and if there be any praise, think on these things.

Your mind could be pre-occupied with these thoughts. The moment you meditate upon anything outside these virtues you will bring your mind under evil control.

ATTACK AGAINST THE MIND

Your mind may be attacked in the following seven ways.

Attack by the forces of Egypt

The forces of Egypt are powers that fight against one's spiritual progress. When Satan and his agents begin to fight against your spiritual progress or spiritual advancement, you are under the attack of the forces of

Egypt. The purpose of such attacks is to revert you back to your unregenerated nature.

The spirit of Egypt may tell you, "You have been born again for ten years and no man has ever proposed marriage to you, why don't you go back to the world? Ladies who are beautiful like you are always in high demand." If you agree with the suggestion, the devil will manufacture a thorough satanic man from the marine kingdom to meet you.

A friend of mine, who happened to be a minister of the gospel, went somewhere to preach and had the most shocking experience of his life. He attracted the anger of an irate mob when he told the people to give their lives to Jesus. They told him to stop mentioning the name of Jesus or face the option of being mobbed to death. He was told; "Leave us alone. We want to serve the devil."

It is very clear that anybody that was trained in the house of the Lord and turns his or her back at God, and goes to serve the devil, or to commercialise the gift of God, will find himself or herself in serious trouble.

The function of the spirit of Egypt is to cause a backward movement. It leads men and women to infantile behaviour.

I am aware of the fact that some members of the MFM are running from one group to another, looking for places of comfort. When such people make up their minds to join a particular group, they are often told: "We have a lot of strict conditions in this place. Such transparent dresses are as good as window blinds"

Such people would run to another group hoping that it will accommodate their transparent dresses. There, they are told, "Sorry madam, we can't admit you as a member of this group, your finger-nails are too long. They look like claws of demons. Why don't you cut them of? " Then the lady may reply, "I cannot part with my finger nails. I have kept them for years." Then they run away from that group to another group where they are told: "Sorry madam, we can't allow people like you to function in this group since we major on deliverance. We simply cannot allow you to put your serpentine chains on." That is how they continue to go from group to group.

Such people are affected by the spirit of Egypt. They may eventually run away from the church. They spend time going from one church to another until they discover that they are not able to find a place that thoroughly meets their needs. Some of them are already coming back to our church.

Forces of repression

Repression is the opposite of expression. To express yourself means to be able to actualise all your goals. The forces of repression work on the mind. Their purpose is to repress the mind. They make people low-spirited, gloomy and despondent. Their primary goal is to sadden and discourage the minds of men and women.

Forces of oppression

Oppressive forces press people down. They lead to worry and anxiety. They make the mind to be bothered by all kinds of things. They bring physical and mental problems to the lives of people. Ninety per cent of church-goers experience one form of oppression or the other. Oppression often leads to obsessions.

Forces of obsession

These forces dominate the lives of people and put men and women under complete control. They cause all kinds of problems for the mind, leading their victims farther away into madness.

When satan is allowed to have complete access to the lives of men or women he goes for total control of their minds. He makes the mind to be totally out of the victim's control. He can cause the mind of the victim to be destroyed physically and spiritually.

FREEDOM FROM THE MADNESS OF THE MIND

How then can we solve the problem of the madness of the mind? What steps must we take to remove every form of malady from the heart?

What must you do if your heart has been invaded by the devil? What scriptural steps and principles must you follow to keep your heart away from evil domination?

Recognise that there is a problem.
Accept the Lord Jesus Christ fully.

Surrender totally to Christ. One fact which you must bear in mind is that every un-surrendered aspect of your life gives room to the devil.

Commit yourself to studying the word of God
Commit yourself completely to the Lord Jesus.
Pray against evil trees.

You must carry out all these steps if you want to have a wholesome mind. Demons know whether you have surrendered yourself to Christ.

A sister came for prayer because she noticed that several things were wrong in her family. She discovered that things began to go haywire as soon as she employed a housemaid. The housemaid was so effective, agile and hard-working that no other one could match her strength and ability.

She woke up at 4.00a.m. in the morning and put everything in the house in order. By the time the family gathered together for quiet time in the morning, she had already prepared breakfast. The husband and the wife were so impressed that they doubled her salary, thinking that they were fortunate to have such a hardworking person in their family.

However, the sister began to notice that everybody in the family began to complain of one ailment or the other. The straw that broke the camel's back was the decision of the maid to attack the sister with her spiritual power.

She did something wrong when the sister was about travelling to England and the sister gave her a few strokes of the cane only to discover that her own hand became swollen within a few minutes. The pain was so unbearable that the sister had to rush to see me.

It took warfare prayers to deal with the problem. We also discovered that there was a problem in the life of the sister which gave the maid an opportunity to attack the members of her family. What happened to her should be a lesson for all careless Christians.

Today, I challenge you to take the following prayer points in order to set your mind free. Say no to madness of the mind. Pray until your mind receives a touch of fire. Then your conscience will receive a divine transformation.

PRAYER POINTS

1. I frustrate every demonic arrest over my mind, in the name of Jesus.

2. Every powerful family spirit and every power of witchcraft working against my life, release me now, in the name of Jesus.

3. Holy Ghost fire, destroy every satanic plantation in my mind, in the name of Jesus.

4. I bind every spirit withstanding my testimony, in the name of Jesus.

5. Every river of backwardness flowing into my mind, dry up, in the name of Jesus.

6. Every evil association with unfriendly friends, break now, in the name of Jesus.

7. I destroy anything that is representing me in any demonic meeting, in the name of Jesus.

3 The Altar of Mind Control

An altar is a structure on which sacrifices are made. It is a place of covenant, physical or spiritual.

The existence of an altar - presupposes the existence of a priest who offers the sacrifices. This gives us a kind of trinity - the altar, the sacrifice and the priest.

As mentioned earlier, there are two types of altar: physical and spiritual. The physical altars are the ones we see all around us while spiritual altars are invisible to the naked eyes and are located mostly in the heavenlies.

The altar that is of concern to us in this chapter is the altar of mind control. This is the altar at which the minds of so many people are controlled with the aim of influencing their thoughts and actions. This is done by certain spirits with demonic powers. To deal with these demonic spirits, we need to be armed with certain facts about life. These facts are contained in the Bible. One

of them can be found in Proverbs 23:7:
For as he thinketh in his heart so is he.

The second fact is found in Proverbs 18:21:
Death and life are in the power of the tongue.

These two passages show that two things shape our lives on earth: our thought and our words. This means that what you are today is a product of what you have been thinking and saying. The Bible tells us that a man who can control his tongue is a perfect man: "For in many things we offend all, if any man offends not in words, the same is a perfect man and also able to bridle his whole body."

Just as the Bible says above, any man who is able to control his tongue will succeed in controlling his whole body. An angry man who decides to allow his tongue to run riot will end up destroying himself as well as other people. Show me a man who speaks as many as 300 words per minute and I will confidently tell you that he will be unwieldy in every part of his life. Talkative persons are miles away from God. This shows us how strong a person's tongue can be and how destructive it can be also when put to wrong use.

In Matthew 12:34a Jesus goes straight to the root of the problem:

O generation of vipers how can ye, being evil, speak good things? For out of the abundance of the heart the mouth speaketh.

Here, we are made to see the heart as the source of all thoughts and words - good and evil. Show me a man whose words are dirty and destructive and I will show you that his heart is corrupt.

If a man approaches me, saying, "I don't know what is going on in my mind, I just don't understand why I find myself thinking evil thoughts all the time." I will know that such a man has a great deal of work to do on his mind.

Then what is the antidote to the problem of the mind? The Bible says: "Thou will keep him in perfect peace whose mind is stayed on thee." You need a divine touch for your mind to be fully delivered. Lasting peace can be your lot only if you can surrender your mind to God. As the above verse says, a heart that is controlled by God experiences great peace. Conversely, a godless mind experiences great trouble and turmoil.

THE EVIL CONTROL

The presence of carnality in the mind makes you God's enemy. To be close to God is to possess a wholesome mind. That is why the Bible says that God has not given us the spirit of fear but of power and of a sound mind. There is no shortcut to possessing a wholesome heart. To have a wholesome mind, you must surrender your heart to God.

All the above, point out the importance of the heart. But while some have been able to keep a sound mind, the minds of so many people remain no better than the devil's workshop: fragmented, confused and deadly. The Bible tells us that there are people who are simply double-minded. These are the minds which the Bible tells us are like the waves of the sea: tossed to and fro and which cannot hope to get anything from the Lord. The Holy Book tells us further: "Keep your heart with all diligence for out of it are the issues of life."

The simple truth is this: Anything that can control your mind will control your thought and, consequently control your words and your actions. At the end, it will control the totality of your life, your destiny inclusive.

To allow your mind to be controlled by bad spirits is to allow yourself to be easily defeated by the devil. It is for this reason that the devil goes for the heart whenever he wants to destroy a man. He knows that with the heart already under his control the person becomes susceptible to his destructive attack.

The devil also knows that God operates from the heart. He therefore tries to corrupt it with a view to making it unsuitable for any form of divine operation. Survey whatever God has done for you in life so far and you will discover that He started from your heart. That is why He declares:

My son give me your heart . . . (Prov 23:26).

The devil, too, is always clamouring for your heart but when you allow him to grab it, he will succeed in controlling your thoughts, words, actions and destiny. It is to achieve this purpose that he has raised up a demonic squad called "mindcontrol spirits." These spirits are meticulous in the discharge of their duties. They have sort of gone nuclear in their operations. Why? The process of controlling a human mind is complex. Their method is by no means haphazard. The finesse required in achieving this satanic goal is possessed by high class demonic agents. It is for the same reason that a qualified surgeon operates with greater precision than a quack.

It is the careful and intelligent spirits that are assigned the task of controlling people's minds. Their expert touch has enabled them to destroy many lives.

THEIR METHOD OF OPERATION

Just how do demonic agents destroy people's lives? The human mind functions like a camera. It takes pictures and develops them in the dark room. The pictures thus developed and kept in the heart may cause problems in the lives of the victims until they are totally destroyed.

Mind control spirits constitute a very powerful family of evil spirits. They form a major force in the army of the devil who constitutes the hidden power behind them. Because of this power behind them, they do not rest until they gain total control of the lives of their victims. It is due to this great power also that they are able to get a lot of lives under their control and influence.

And how do these evil influences manifest in people's lives?

They prevent people from thinking clearly: A lot of people come to me to complain of hearing strange voices that prevent them from thinking clearly. This is the handiwork of evil controllers.

The inability to concentrate during prayers

A lot of people are unable to continue in their prayer immediately they feel something strike their heart. Such a disturbance may sound ordinary but it has deeper meaning and effect.

To fully appreciate this, imagine yourself about to make an important point during a telephone conversation and just then you are distracted to the extent that you suddenly drop the phone while the person at the other end keeps hanging on and wondering if you are still there. By the time you are through with the distraction and get back to the phone to resume the conversation you find that the other person has dropped the receiver after he had run out of patience waiting for you. It may not be very easy for you to reach the person again.

A lot of people are unable to continue in their prayer when they get to the stage where they notice an evil presence. They lose their focus and most of the time go back to square one.

Insanity problem

These mind control spirits are also responsible for most of the insanity or mental illnesses that occur in the society.

Feeling of looming death

A lot of people go about with the feeling that they could collapse and die any moment. A lot of them also receive dangerous compulsive instructions.

For example, when they see on-coming vehicles, something tells them to jump into the middle of the road. It is also the mind control spirits that urge a person to swallow a whole bottle of valium tablets.

Recently, a professor of mathematics was attacked by demonic mind controllers who made him lose his sense of reasoning. The attack was not too pronounced initially. However, as time went on, he would stop abruptly in the middle of a conversation with his colleagues, would bend down and begin to work mathematics on the ground with his fingers. Sometimes he would work mathematics verbally in the middle of a conversation. At other times, especially when alone, he would work mathematics on the windscreen of his car.

When things went on this way with the professor for a long while, it became clear that he had lost the control of his mind. Before anything could be done for him, he had put his 16-year-old housemaid in the family way. That was how his life was ruined by demonic mind controllers.

Confused male/female relationship

Mind controllers also work to destroy male/female relationships. I have had occasion to warn female members of our church not to marry certain unconverted gentlemen. Most of them disregarded my warning with the hope that they would be able to convert their suitors.

Often, because of their desperation to get married, some even go to the extent of avoiding me in order to actualise their self-wish. Unknown to most of them, they are victims of demonic mind-controllers that get them married to alcoholics and chain-smokers.

More than at any other time in human history, mind-controlling spirits are at their worst in their work in people's lives. Occult groups now advertise in dailies or magazines. Some groups in India now place adverts on charms, amulets, rings and love potions for unsuspecting young men and women. Their method of operation is to invite young men to buy special powder with which to charm a lady of their choice.

They also, advertise rings that they claim have the power to protect the wearers from accidents or attacks by armed robbers. In this way, many gullible young people have fallen victims of these demonic manipulators.

A lot of men and women actually avoid immorality but find it difficult to control themselves whenever they come in contact with certain persons. Through the manipulation of these demonic agents, evil thoughts bombard their minds day and night until they are no longer able to resist the urge to commit immorality.

When mind-control spirits gain access to a person's photograph they can use it to influence and control the person. Also, a person's hair can be used to direct his affairs. For example, they can afflict a person with a terrible headache by using his hair. They would light a candle and begin to pour its hot wax on the hair until their victim begins to suffer a great headache. The person may eventually die as a result of the headache. Black candles can also be used to compel victims to commit suicide. The black candle is a terrible satanic weapon. Manipulations to lust and immoralities are also achieved with it.

If you have ever submitted your photograph to fetish priests or false prophets, you must pray the following prayer points with all seriousness.

If your shoes, head gears, under-wears or clothes have, at one time or the other, disappeared mysteriously, you need to pray with all your strength.

Also, if you have ever made the mistake of giving your picture to an occult boyfriend, you stand the risk of having your mind controlled negatively.

Close this book for a moment and take this prayer point: **Any symbol used against me in the demonic world, I withdraw you by fire, in the name of Jesus.**

From the foregoing, you can see that mind-controlling spirits are wicked and can do a lot of havoc in people's lives. To be able to determine the extent to which they have influenced your thoughts and actions in the past, you may need to run your mind through certain unpleasant situations you have passed through in recent or distant times.

If you are able to remember any, can you identify it as an evidence of the activities of mind-controllers in your life? Even at present, do you feel that your mind is under the attack of evil spirits?

Are you losing your mind gradually? In what way are evil spirits destroying your mind?

You must never take anything for granted. You must deal squarely with all mind controlling spirits as soon as you notice their presence in your life.

PRAYER POINTS

Make the following confessions out loud:

O Lord, it is written that even the lawful captive shall be delivered. Therefore, I decree today, according to your word, that every lawful bondage in my life be broken, in the name of Jesus.

You water spirit, hear the word of the Lord, I have given my life to Jesus the Lord. You have no authority over me again. Therefore, I bring the rebuke of the Lord upon you. I anchor your head to divine judgement, in the name of Jesus.

It is written, henceforth, let no man trouble me for I bear in my body the mark of the Lord Jesus Christ. I am crucified with Christ. Every handwriting contrary to my life must be nailed to the cross.

Therefore, I break every dedication to water spirits. Any blood or water pollution in my body, come out by fire. I destroy every record of marine powers kept against my destiny in the marine world, and I redeem myself by the blood of Jesus.

Jesus is my original spouse and He is jealous over me. Therefore, I issue a bill of divorcement to every spirit husband/wife, in the name of Jesus. Every spirit husband/wife, I bind you with everlasting chains, in the name of Jesus.

1. Every evil record fashioned against me, blood of Jesus, wipe it off, in the name of Jesus.

2. Any evil rope on my loins, be broken, in Jesus' name.

3. I come against every marine spirit by the word of the Lord, in the name of Jesus.

4. Every marine certificate, be burnt, in the name of Jesus.

5. You marine power, release every good thing that belongs to me which you are holding under bondage, in the name of Jesus.

6. I pronounce a divine jubilee upon my life, in Jesus' name.

7. O Lord, increase my strength for warfare today, in the name of Jesus.

8. I ride on the horse of war today, in the name of Jesus.

9. O Lord, let your arrow be strong against the heart of my enemy today, in the name of Jesus.

10. I arrest the horse, the chariots and the horsemen of marine powers, in the name of Jesus.

11. I frustrate the token of marine powers, in Jesus' name.

12. You demonic river, release my virtues, in Jesus' name.

13. You marine power, I command your diviners to become mad right now, in the name of Jesus.

14. Every area of co-operation with water spirits, I command you to be broken today, in the name of Jesus.

15. Every ancestral covenant with water spirits, break, in the name of Jesus.

16. Every deposit of water spirit in my life, be flushed out by the blood of Jesus.

17. I release myself from every sex trap, in Jesus' name.

18. Any spiritual plan contrary to the Holy Ghost, I reject you, in the name of Jesus.

19. You spirit husband/wife, I burn your certificate and I destroy your ring, in the name of Jesus.

20. Let every evil spirit spouse hear this announcement: I bear in my body the mark of the Lord Jesus. Every sin of fornication on my body that has been written with an iron pen, I wipe you off, in the name of Jesus.

21. Every trademark of water spirits, be shaken out of my life, in the name of Jesus.

22. I bring the blood of Jesus against all the spirits that do not want me to go.

23. For every report made against me by the wicked spirits, I file a counter report against it, in the name of Jesus.

24. Every satanic exhibit, tendered against me, be destroyed by fire, in the name of Jesus.

25. My redeemer is my maker and He is my husband, in the name of Jesus.

26. O Lord, defend Your interest in my life, in Jesus' name.

4 Mind Controlling Spirits

As mentioned in the previous chapter, a man is a product of two things: his thoughts and his words. According to Proverbs 23:7,
For as he thinketh in his heart, so is he.

Thoughts and words work hand in hand.

In Proverbs 18:21, we read:
Death and life are in the power of the tongue.

If the Scripture says, "As a man thinketh so is he," and that "Death and life are in the power of the tongue," this means that these two things combined, determine what a person will be. Automatically, what you are today is a by-product of what you have been thinking and saying in the past. This is why James 3 tells us that the ability to control your tongue is a mark of perfection.

If you read the whole of James chapter 3, you will discover how powerful the tongue is. The moment you are able to control it, you are able to control any other thing concerning your life.

The Lord Jesus delved into the matter, in Matthew 12:34-35 where He tells us:
O generation of vipers, how can ye, being evil, speak good things? For out of abundance of heart the mouth speaketh. A good man out of the good treasure of the heart bringeth forth good things: and evil man out of the evil treasure bringeth forth evil things.

We can see that the Lord Jesus spared no effort in making us realise that before the tongue begins to operate in a bad way the heart must have been filthy. It is out of the abundant filthiness of the heart that man speaks out dirty things. So, a proud heart would speak out proud things and a heart of unbelief would speak out unbelief. The problem with wrong speaking is that it gets right down your lungs.

Isaiah 26:3, is that very popular verse,
Thou wilt keep him in perfect peace, whose mind is stayed on thee.

This means that the qualification for being kept in perfect peace is for the heart to be stayed on God.

In Mark 5:15, Jesus healed a very aggressive person. After the healing, the Bible has this to say:
And they come to Jesus, and see him that was possessed with the devil, and had the legion, sitting and clothed, and in his right mind: and they were afraid.

So the reason the man was getting violent, tearing himself with rocks and inflicting himself with pains was that his mind was wrong. And Romans 8:6 tells us:
For to be carnally minded is death; but to be spiritually minded is life and peace.

I have brought all these into focus again so that we can clearly see the influence of the mind on all that a man does.

Galatians 1:21-23 tells us:
Afterwards I came into the regions of Syria and Cilicia; and was unknown by face unto the churches of Judea which were in Christ: but they had heard only, That he which persecuted us in times past now preacheth the faith which once he destroyed.

That was the testimony of Apostle Paul when his mind was changed. They glorified God for him. And if we read

II Timothy 1:7 we find that well-known Scripture which says:
For God hath not given us the spirit of fear; but of power, and of love, and of a sound mind.

The above verse shows us that it is possible for a man to have the spirit of an unsound mind. Again, II Corinthians 11:3 tells us:
But I fear, lest by any means, as the serpent beguiled Eve through his subtilty, so your minds should be corrupted from the simplicity that is in Christ.

This verse tells us that a person's mind can be corrupted.

And in James 1:8, we also read that:
A double-minded man is unstable in all his ways.

This brings us to the main topic of this chapter. Anything that can control the mind of a man will definitely control his thoughts, and once it is able to control his thoughts, it will control his words, and once it is able to control his words, it will begin to control his actions. And when it starts to control his actions, it controls his life. So, every problem starts from the mind.

Even when you want to meet God, everything starts from the mind also. If bad spirits can control the mind of a person, the person is easily defeated. Just as victory starts in the mind, defeat too starts in the mind.

What we refer to as mind control spirits belong to the powerful family of evil spirits. They are often the hidden strength behind other spirits that operate and are important weapons used by the enemy against the soul.

A lot of minds are under the control and activities of these mind control spirits, and if this problem is not checked on time it will lead to demonic possession, or demonic domination, or what we refer to as being bewitched.

Mind control spirits, too, give satanic agents the ability to control other people.

They prevent people from thinking clearly.

They are responsible for causing noises in people's heads.

They are responsible for lack of concentration during prayer.

They cause insanity and other mental illnesses.

They initiate the thought of dying.

They also make people to believe that they will become poor if they leave a dead church.

All the unreasonable intellectualism is under the control of mind control spirits. Sometimes when a person runs mad gradually, people attribute it to his deep knowledge of mathematics rather than send him for prompt deliverance. And when the "learned fellow" begins to run after his maid at night then they forget about mathematics and charge him to court.

When it comes to male-female relationship, a lot of single people behave as if their brains were under their feet. This is not their fault; they are under the influence of the mind control spirits. This often makes them insist on marrying wrong partners in spite of advice and entreaties against this. Mind control spirits blind their eyes against reason and they are unable to think clearly.

5 The Dangerous Mind Demons

You can never experience what it takes to have good conscience unless you pay attention to the state of your mind. The mind is the seat of all emotions. A faulty mind will lead to a faulty conscience.

Therefore, if you allow demons to feast on your mind they would turn your conscience into their own habitation. The loss that could be experienced by that kind of conscience is incalculable. A lot of terrible things will happen. The victim will not be able to hold himself together. This state will lead to several physical and spiritual sicknesses.

Many people do not know that there are lots of dangerous mind demons around. These mind demons are daily seeking new preys. Whenever they discover a good landing spot in the life of any one they quickly take advantage of it. In the world, today, certain dangerous mind demons are perpetrating all kinds of havocs.

The only problem is that the victims of such attacks do not know the source or the origin of their problems. They only know that they are battling with serious sickness, deep psychological problems, acute depression, stress, negative mood, long standing sicknesses, nightmares and all kinds of problems which medical science know little or nothing about. They hardly link what they are going through with the wicked activities of some unseen demons which attack the human mind.

The devil on his own knows what he is doing. He knows that the only way he can capture his victims is to affect their consciences through their minds quietly but meticulously, not minding how long it takes him to succeed. He has a goal: to destroy as many lives as possible through the mind. The battle that takes place in the arena of the human conscience is one which you cannot afford to lose.

Therefore, I challenge you to prepare yourself spiritually by taking the following prayer points:

Today, I must possess my possession, in the name of Jesus.

O thou that troubleth my Israel my God shall trouble you today, in the name of Jesus.

Every Pharaoh of poverty, die, in the name of Jesus.

Every Pharaoh of backwardness, die, in the name of Jesus;

If you know the volume of traffic that goes on in the mind you will see the need for more concentration on efforts towards the decongestion of negative luggage.

Recently, I read two news items in one of the dailies which set me thinking. The first news item was on a story of a jilted lady who set herself ablaze. The second story was on a man who drank acid because of his state of mind. The two stories made a host of questions to flood my mind. I asked,

"What must have been going on in the minds of those people? What really disturbed or affected their emotional balance to the point that they decided to terminate their lives abruptly? What fearful power troubled their minds? What kind of dark force was ruling their minds? How could anything disturb somebody's mind to the extent of making the fellow to swallow acid? Why should a woman decide to set herself ablaze as if no man would ever make a proposal to her?"

These questions made me to discover the fact that the human mind is the fiercest battle arena.

The human mind is a delicate instrument. It can be rendered unsound by many things. God knows that the human mind is prone to attacks. That is why he has provided a divine immunity. This is stated very clearly in 2Tim. 1:7: "For God hath not given us the spirit of fear; but of power, and of love, and of a sound mind."

A sound mind can only be achieved through divine grace. It is a glorious possibility which can be received by those who allow God to affect their minds positively. Unfortunately, the minds of so many people are far from being sound.

Several people fall into the category of those whose state of mind is difficult to detect. We will hardly understand the state of the human mind except we watch people's actions. But for the occasional misdemeanors which strike us as irrational, we may not know that many friends and neighbours go about with sick minds. It is tragic that no scientist has discovered a device which detects or analyses the problems of the human mind.

Many people get to a state where things go haywire when they would have done something to nip their problems in the bud. Again, we cannot blame them. This is simply because majority do not know what is happening in the arena of their minds. If someone can take a picture of the state of the mind of every human being, most people would have decided to solve such mind- related problems at their infancy.

I don't know any secular book which explains the activities of evil powers in the territory of the mind. Psychologists do not even know of the existence of demons whose field of operation is the human mind. This kind of ignorance explains why things are approached from the surface level. Nothing is done to address the depth of the root of all mind-related problems.

Right now, you may not even know what is going on at the altar of your mind. If the one who owns that mind is ignorant, what about neighbours and colleagues? This general ignorance accounts for why the devil has continued to launch terrible attacks against the mind.

There is no denying the fact that the devil has mastered the art of using our minds against us. He has discovered a lot of cheap tools which he has continued to use to destroy lives.

For example, bad health can lead the mind into terrible thoughts. Immediately some people get sick they begin to dream about death. Some people meditate on songs that are generally rendered during burial ceremonies. Bad health can, therefore, turn the human mind into a troubled spot.

Again, the human mind can be affected by hereditary behaviours. Many people worry simply because such habits can be found in its highest degree in their family line. If those who worry excessively examine the lives of their parents or ancestors, they would discover that such people were worry bags too.

The human mind can be attacked by old age. Human physiology depreciates with age due to the wear and tear of life. When people get older, their minds may no longer be as active and sharp as it was in their younger years. As most people grow older, their mental sharpness drops. Those who become very old generally become senile. Some people get to the point where they begin to behave like little children.

It is strange, however, that whenever an old man decides to commit sin, his mind may no longer be senile. Senility or old age only affects such people when they are expected to do what is good.

Our thoughts would like to run riots without any inhibition. It would like to wander without being challenged. If the mind is allowed to wander the way it likes, anything can happen.

Do you know that there is a dangerous evil spirit which has made the human heart or the mind its headquarters? This demon has perpetrated a lot of destruction in these last days. This is one destructive spirit that has down-graded and destroyed millions of destinies.

The mind is the factory or the laboratory of the evil spirit. The major preoccupation of this spirit is to attack concentration. It specializes in attacking the ability of the mind to pay attention. Once this spirit begins to attack, you will have difficulty paying attention. It is a very clever spirit. This is not an illiterate demon.

If you are really honest with yourself, you will own up the fact that you sometimes experience lack of concentration. This sometimes happens in schools or classrooms, during church services and during important private, business or social conversations. This problem often gets to a serious dimension, when people no longer find it easy to fix their minds on what they are being told.

Some people blank off for minutes only to recover themselves after important statements have been made. Some people experience such problems even while working. Others are affected when they are praying or studying the Bible. For such people, the ability to focus suddenly disappears.

Many are unable to hold their thoughts together. Lack of ability to pay attention may last for such a long time that the victim becomes disjointed emotionally. In some terrible cases, it happens when some people are in the midst of important conversation, the listener will become embarrassed.

This reminds me of someone who stood before a crowd to lead them in a praise worship session. He became publicly embarrassed as he forgot all the songs he had made up his mind to sing. He was attacked by a dangerous mind demon.

These dangerous mind demons attack the concentration of the mind. When a person's attention is attacked in this manner, it results in an emotional imbalance. At that point, the person may not be able to move forward in deep and meaningful thinking. Experts have given a scientific name to this. It is called autism, otherwise known as mind-blindness.

According to a report in 'The Newsweek', an American magazine, issue of July 31, 2000, "More kids than ever are facing the challenge of 'mind blindness'. The cause is still a mystery, but research is offering new clues to how the brain works."

Such a problem is characterized by screaming instead of sleeping at night, unnecessary reaction even to body contact with clothes. When autistic children grow up they continue to battle with mental defects with that kind of terrible disorder.

It is unfortunate that scientists have no solution to the problem of mind blindness. The use of tranquilizers and anti-depressants has not helped matters. Any effort or solution that falls short of identifying and dealing with dangerous mind demons cannot put a check on the activities of the spirit behind mind blindness.

The problems of mind blindness or stress can be found in the lives of children and adults. Some experience it at the point of birth; for others, it develops when they are getting to adulthood.

Sometimes, it appears suddenly without any previous history of instability of the mind. For some, it happens at specific periods. It happens in the lives of some other people when they are under serious stress or trauma. It often happens to some people when they are surrounded by a crowd. Such people suffer from what is called crowd fright. For some it happens only in the morning. By evening time, it would have disappeared. Some people are normal at the beginning of the week but they experience mind blankness when they are approaching weekend.

There are lots of mysterious problems in the world. However, the Bible has given us the prescription concerning how to deal with such problems. 2 Cor. 10:3-5 says:

For though we walk in the flesh, we do not war after the flesh: [4](For the weapons of our warfare are not carnal, but mighty through God to the pulling down of strong holds;) [5]Casting down imaginations, and every high thing that exalteth itself against the knowledge

of God, and bringing into captivity every thought to the obedience of Christ;

The heart is the place where thoughts and imaginations make their abode. The devil uses imagination and thoughts to introduce confusion and all kinds of physical and spiritual problems into the lives of men, women and children.

But the Bible tells us that we should look beyond the physical realm and focus on the spirit realm. What we experience while we walk in the flesh should not make us to battle with our physical abilities. We should resort to the use of spiritual weapons to deal with all negative strongholds attacking our minds. Definite efforts must be made towards casting down imaginations and capturing every thought until we subject the totality of what goes on in our minds to the obedience of Christ. We must not allow just any baggage to be deposited on the altar of our minds.

Philipians 4:8 carefully outlines the kind of things we should allow in the territory of our minds. These things should be carefully weighed as they are the only things that would keep our minds healthy. It says:

Finally, brethren, whatsoever things are true, whatsoever things are honest, whatsoever things are just, whatsoever things are pure, whatsoever things are lovely, whatsoever things are of good report; if there be any virtue, and if there be any praise, think on these things.

Can you truly say that what can be found in your mind are:

- ✓ Honest
- ✓ Just
- ✓ Pure
- ✓ Lovely
- ✓ Of good report
- ✓ Virtuous
- ✓ Praise worthy
- ✓ True

Again if what can be found in your mind are exact opposites of the aforesaid things, then you must go through the deliverance of the mind. If you are thinking about things that are dishonest, unjust, impure, dirty, scandalous, uncomely, false, and things that attract condemnation, your mind has been invaded by dangerous mind demons.

The principle of pure thinking and profitable meditation is practically known to many people, especially Africans. Meditation is very profitable and beneficial. It brings revelation, and when it does so, you will be guided aright. Proper direction, on the other hand, will lead to success. Everything boils down to meditation.

This is stated very clearly in Joshua 1:8:
This book of the law shall not depart out of thy mouth; but thou shalt meditate therein day and night, that thou mayest observe to do according to all that is written therein: for then thou shalt make thy way prosperous, and then thou shalt have good success.

The greatest problem that can be found in the lives of many people, today, is largely due to inability to carry out meaningful meditation.

The problem of inability to meditate far surpasses the problems of spirit husband and spirit wife. It is much more serious than being under witchcraft attack. If you discover that your mind cannot concentrate on the word of God it is an indication of the fact that your heart has been invaded by dangerous mind demons.

If your meditation falls short of securing honey from the word of God, your mind is under an evil invasion: you have a serious problem. Some people's hearts are so noisy that they resort to playing loud music to neutralize the effects of their inner turmoil. Herein lies one of the greatest problems of spiritual maturity and growth.

In our present society, even in Christendom, very few people engage in profitable and deep thinking. Very few are able to benefit from the spiritual exercise called meditation. This is undoubtedly one of the greatest problems that have bedeviled the black race.

For example, an African would spend time thinking about spending millions on buying exquisite cars without giving consideration to the availability of good roads in rural areas where he hopes to travel to very often. While the whites are busy exploring other planets, many Africans are struggling with how to cope with the rising cost of cassava granules.

<>Few of us are actually involved in profitable thinking. Some of us are busy blaming the weather for our inability to achieve great scientific feats. That is an empty excuse. There is no sense in it. Our weather is

both warm and friendly. We have one of the best weathers in the world. Many people live under the bridge. If you ever do that in Canada you will be frozen to death. Most countries in Africa have a good balance of beautiful, warm and cool weather. We are supposed to be very productive. Our lack of productivity and achievement can be traced to a demonic invasion by terrible local mind demons.

Until we conquer the problems introduced by dangerous mind demons, we may not be able to engage in profitable thinking. Blacks may continue to trail behind the whites until useless activities and past times are abandoned for profitable thinking. We need to wake up. If the Christian population in Africa can deal decisively with these evil mind demons, we will be able to move the continent forward.

Thinking can be a useful or dangerous occupation. It is capable of leading the thinker into negative or positive achievement. The enemy does not want us to think positively. Do you know that those who have dangerous demons in their minds find it difficult to concentrate even when they are praying? Therefore, one of the greatest enemies of prayer is wandering thoughts.

The devil hates to see you pray. That is why he tries to divert your attention. Some people may shout or scream prayer points with their mouths while their minds are thousands of kilometers away. If a demon is attacking your mind, you need to bind it and cast it out today.

A prayer warrior is someone who can maintain his focus and prayerfully concentrate on what he is praying about with spiritual energy. The inability to focus one's energy on prayer accounts for several cases of unanswered prayers today. Prayer without concentration cannot stop the evil tide. How can you say that you are praying seriously when buying and selling is seriously going on in your mind? The human mind cannot be a prayer altar and a busy marketplace at the same time.

How can you say that you are praying when you don't even understand what you are praying about? If you pray with a doubtful mind, you may not know what it means to experience the result of fervent praying. A lot of what goes on in the name of praying can be categorized under worrying, anxiety, day dreaming and business activities.

The enemy with whom we are contending is a clever enemy. He is so wicked and bad in a superlative sense.

He will not spare you a moment for fruitful concentration. Deep meditation is the only activity that can lead you to breakthrough. You cannot come across gold on the floor. It is deeply buried underneath the earth. You must dig very deep to get it.

The mystery of God cannot be found on the surface by those whose efforts are concentrated on trivialities. If you desire to receive deep things from the Lord you must dig very deep. Therefore, the wandering heart cannot operate in the office of the prayer warrior. Such a person would belong to the group of prayer warriors and intercessors but he is not part of them.

The conscience or the mind should be fenced off from all attacks of dangerous mind demons. Whenever the devil wants to attack your mind, he places it in a cooler. His intention is to subject it to attacks until everything gets to a freezing point. When the heart or the mind has been frozen, it is no longer alive.

Sin can be likened to the refrigerator. The longer your heart stays there the more hardened it becomes. This explains why a lot of people are so insensitive to the voice of the Spirit. The devil, therefore, first makes the heart dead before going further. In that dead stage, dangerous mind demons are invited to conclude the work of destruction which the devil sets out to do.

The activities of dangerous mind demons are so serious that it is risky to allow the heart to remain their prey. Mind demons do not need so much time to lead their victims into the land of destruction. Once they are given a short time to carry out the evil activities, they quickly conclude the assignment.

SIGNS OF DANGEROUS MIND DEMONS

You may ask, how can I really ascertain whether I am a victim of the activities of dangerous mind demons? That is a very good question. You need to run your heart through serious diagnosis if you must wrestle it from the hands of these destructive demons. The following are examples of how to identify the activities of serious mind demons:

- **Regular experience of mind blankness**
  When this happens to you, your mind will suddenly become blank and it will take you a while to recollect yourself.

- **Unprofitable forgetfulness**
  You may be amazed that you are always forgetting what you are expected to remember. Even if you were very intelligent, you would find yourself forgetting important details. You will always remember worldly slang or slogans while you will find it difficult to remember important passages of the Scripture. You may not remember important passages which contain solutions to your problems.

- **Memory loss**
  This happens for instance, when people get to the examination hall and find it difficult to remember what they studied previously. Those who are fond of telling lies often suffer this. They contradict themselves when they have forgotten the previous lies they told. The new lies which they told in order to cover up embarrassingly contradict the lies they told before.

- **Brain fatigue**
  This borders on the tiredness of the brain. It will make you to manifest characteristics of dullness. When the brain gets to the point that is fagged out, its functions, will begin to depreciate.

- **Inability to absorb information**
  You can speak with some people for an hour without succeeding to make them grasp the details of what you are saying. Such people are under severe attack.

- **Dream eraser**
  This is a very powerful weapon which the enemy uses to lead multitudes into confusion. Whenever this power attacks you, you will begin to forget your dream on regular basis. You may know that the dream which you had is important but it will vanish mysteriously. You are under the attack of an evil spirit called 'dream-eraser'. The devil knows that when he makes you to forget all your dreams you will not know the direction to which God is leading you.

- **Inability to focus**
  If you have discovered that you lack the ability to focus your attention on important things you are under the attack of dangerous mind demons. If you pick up some activities and assignments, pursue them for a while, abandon them and pick up others, leave them half way and you are not able to hold on to anything, this is as a result of the fact that you are under the influence of demons that hinder

people from concentration or lead them into lack of focus.

- **Inability to concentrate**

  These can come in various forms. Some people cannot concentrate when they are praying while others find it difficult to concentrate when they are studying the word of God. Most problems in life require serious concentration before one can achieve solutions.

  For example, if you are able to concentrate for ten minutes, you will discover the solution fast. Some people come to me saying, "Man of God, what is happening to me? I have handled all the prayer points you gave me, but I don't seem to have achieved any result."

  Others say, "I have prayed 200 prayer points within one hour." Those who make such claims do not really concentrate during such so-called prayer sessions. Their minds were busy going from one place to another. How can you say you have handled prayer points effectively when your mind is busy going from one country to another? You must be able to achieve a total focus in prayer.

Prayer is addressed to the God of heaven and earth. You cannot afford to be haphazard in prayer.

For example, if you are told to address the president of the nation and you say something like, "Mr. President, I am glad to bring my requests before you, don't mind the tempo of my voice, I am down with some migraine. How do you even cope with ruling this nation? Mr. President, do you know that I never thought I could stand face to face before you? Mr. President, do you know that I need a good pair of shoes? Before I continue with my request, let me commend your statesmanship. By the way, Mr. President, let me ask you a question. Okay, before I ask the question, don't forget my pair of shoes, O, I have just remembered, I am actually here to represent a group of people. I have even forgotten what I have been mandated to tell you, Mr. President, I want you to pardon me, sir, I have just forgotten what I wanted to say next. In any case, thank you Mr. President for the privilege of having an audience with you."

The president would simply wonder why the fellow has decided to come to waste his precious time. Why should someone trifle with such precious opportunity?

- **Roaming mind**
  Some people's minds are never stable. They roam all the corners of the globe. The devil knows that once you concentrate you will achieve much. He therefore makes your mind to roam about. Those whose minds roam about cannot know what it means to experience fervency in prayer. Fervent prayer must be said with fire and concentration.

- **Lack of Focus on one's thought system**
  You can spend an hour thinking without achieving focus for one minute.

- **Vagabond spirit in prayer**
  When you spend precious time in prayer but your mind wanders like a vagabond, your effort will end in futility.

- **Divided mind**
  The Bible addresses this problem in James 1:6-8: "But let him ask in faith, nothing wavering. For he that wavereth is like a wave of the sea driven with the wind and tossed. 7For let not that man think that he shall receive any thing of the Lord. 8A double minded man is unstable in all his ways."

- **Mind confusion**
  The minds of many people are totally destabilized and confused. Whenever this kind of problem goes on in anybody's mind, the victim will not know how to gather his thoughts together.

- **Attention deficiency**
  Many people are hardly ever able to retain attention during conversation or while listening to somebody. And many minds are so restless that their ability to concentrate is zero.

- **Thought scattering**
  This happens when the mind is fragmented and is unable to gather things together.

- **Meditation deficiency**
  Those who are attacked in this area find it difficult to meditate on the word of God.

- **Mind blocking**
  In this case, the mind is suddenly blocked and the free flow of thought is hindered

- **Deadness of the mind**
  The mind will not be able to carry out meaningful operation.

- **Dryness of the mind**
  It is possible for someone's mind to dry up completely. This kind of mind is devoid of every freshness. It is characterized by serious poverty of ideas. There is really no financial poverty, the problem is poverty of ideas. If you have a good idea, you will surely experience prosperity.

  It can be terrible when these forces join hands together to attack a single mind. The effect of such a massive and multiple attack can be very destructive. You may ask how do people become victims of these kinds of terrible attack? Let me give you a run down of some of these causes:

- **Through inheritance**
  A lot of these things are inherited. Some parents pass these problems to their offspring. Hence some of them travel down generational lines.

- **Mental laziness**
  Mental laziness has led a lot of people into serious problems. Some people are so lazy that they are not ready to think for themselves. They expect those who are around them to do for them whatever borders on serious thinking.

- **Curses**

  Many mind-related problems originate from all kinds of curses. Many of us do not know what our ancestors did wrong. Many of them were cursed down to their generations. A curse could take a hundred years to attain maturity. The moment it attains maturity, somebody may wake up suddenly with a serious mind problem.

  For example, if somebody receives the curse of poverty, such a person may never succeed in thinking about ideas that will lead him to a breakthrough. His thoughts will become scattered or disjointed.

- **Fear and anxiety**

  Many mind or conscience related problems emanate from fear and anxiety.

- **Guilty conscience**

  The moment your mind is bothered by guilt, your thoughts will be affected. A serious battle will begin in your mind. The result can be very catastrophic.

- **Addiction to sleep**
  A lot of people cannot enjoy the benefit of a wholesome mind because they are addicted to sleep. Such people can sleep for 10 hours in a single day. Even when they are awake, their minds are still sleeping. Some people fall asleep just when a brilliant idea is coming up on their minds and may never remember such beneficial ideas.

HOW TO DEAL WITH DANGEROUS MIND DEMONS

The important question is, how can we deal with this dangerous demon?

Acknowledge the fact that there is a problem. Don't sweep your problem under the carpet. Own it up.

- **Believe that a sound mind is a possibility**
  It is your birth-right. No matter what has happened in the past, you are entitled to have and enjoy a sound mind.

- **Declare all curses against your mind broken and nullified**
  You must address them because they are responsible for all the mind problems you have been going through.

- **Submit your mind to God's word and to the Holy Spirit**

- **Introduce spiritual discipline into your mind**
  Do not allow your mind to be turned into a theater of war. Let there be order, decency and decorum there. Refuse to allow your thought to go on a rampage. Let your mind have divine discipline. Decide that your thought must act only under your center. You can and you must choose the kind of thought you want. If a particular thought, sounds unpleasant to you, get rid of it instantly.

- **Begin daily scriptural meditation**
  Memorize the scriptures and use them daily. Read the bible through in one year. This must be done in a systematic manner. An average Christian who has been born again for a period of five years is supposed to memorize a minimum of 52 memory verses.

There are Christians who can be labeled prayer point factories but exhibit poverty when it comes to the word of God. Such people are wasting their time. The devil will always attack such people.

- **Decide to be the immigration officer at the gateway of your mind**

  The mind has a number of gateways. These include:
  The eye.
  The ear.
  The memory.
  The habit.

  You should watch over these four gates. You should only allow the thoughts that carry legal divine passport to gain entrance. Any other thought that runs contrary to the will of God must be sent packing.

- **Destroy by fire every evil possession in your habitation**

  Fire is the only solution to all kinds of unwanted demonic invasions.

- **Carry out serious deliverance programme on your heart**

  Your mind needs serious deliverance. You cannot enjoy your benefits on earth without running your mind through serious deliverance. If you examine what has happened to you so far you would have discovered that a lot of evil materials have been deposited on your mind. You must undergo spiritual environmental sanitation. This will rid your life of all dangerous mind demons. Examine how you have allowed the demon of destruction to gain access into your spirit. How is your level of concentration?

  At this point, I want you to recall the parable of the sower. We are told that the seeds that fell on the wayside were picked up by the birds of the air. The birds of the air are evil birds that attack the mind. They pick up profitable things from the mind of a man. The internal enemy is the most dangerous of all. Many people will continue to be poor until they introduce discipline into their thoughts while many will not receive the powers which they are asking God until they introduce discipline into their personal meditation.

You may remain impoverished spiritually until you wage war against all dangerous mind demons. You will never experience the kind of change which you are expecting unless you carry out fierce battle against all contrary spirits that have turned your mind to a battle arena. You will have to cast down all demonic imaginations troubling your mind.

You must also pull down every demonic stronghold if you must move forward. If you don't deal with dangerous mind demons, your prayer effort will yield no dividend. Why do you allow a defeatist attitude to rule your mind? If your mind is not focused on your destiny, you may not move far. No wonder the Bible says, "The heart of man is desperately wicked. Who can know it?" I counsel you to handle the following prayer points with all seriousness they deserve.

PRAYER POINTS

1. Every arrow of witchcraft fired into my mind, come out, in the name of Jesus.

2. Let the blood of Jesus purge my mind, in Jesus' name.

3. Thou power of darkness targeted against my mind, what are you waiting for? Die, in the name of Jesus.

4. Every familiar spirit trading in the temple of my heart, die, in the name of Jesus.

5. Return unto thy resting place, O my heart, in Jesus' name.

6. Every personal witchcraft cage troubling my mind break in the name of Jesus.

7. Every power working against my concentration during prayer, what are you waiting for? Die in the name of Jesus.

6 Deliverance of The Mind

As a prelude to this chapter, I would like you to close your eyes and take this prayer point:

"Let any strongman delegated to monitor my life be paralysed, in the name of Jesus."

A lot of people have continued to light fake fires while leaving the real fire in their lives unquenched. Such people are eternally complaining: "I wonder why nothing seems to be working for me. I wonder why I have not achieved any tangible thing, in spite of the several methods I have adopted to solve my problems."

The truth is that such people are yet to realize that it is possible to spend the whole of one's lifetime applying the wrong method to solve a particular problem. But, no matter how hard they try, they are not likely to achieve any victory as long as they continue to use the wrong method.

Using a wrong method can be likened to a man who finds himself moving towards the west when he is supposed to be heading eastward. Even when such a person is seen to be making a lot of physical movements he will ultimately end up at the wrong end of his journey, regardless of what efforts, money, time and energy are expended in the process. If you focus on the wrong target you will end up being worse than a failure in life.

It is quite unfortunate that most people spend their energy on non-essentials instead of focusing on life's priorities. They concentrate all their physical and spiritual energies on things that are inconsequential as far as eternity is concerned. Anyone who falls into this bracket can be likened to a footballer who decides to play his own game outside the football pitch. No matter how skillful or agile he may be, nobody will take notice of him. The relevance of a footballer is only in the football field.

God wants us to concentrate our attention on the true condition of our hearts. But it is unfortunate that many children of God are busy concentrating on worldly things. If you continue to occupy yourself with trivial matters, you will end up receiving condemnation from God.

Many believers are in trouble today because of their lack of attention to the state of their hearts. The more you take care of the state of your heart, the more wholesome your life will become.

If you spray your room with insecticide and at the same time leave the doors and the windows open for mosquitoes to come in, you will, sooner or later, discover that you have not solved any problem. Even though the mosquitoes may lie low for a while, immediately the effect of the insecticide subsides, they will come back to torment you. The only permanent solution, therefore, lies in keeping the doors and windows of your house shut before you deal with the mosquitoes. Or, if you must keep the doors and windows open, fix nets on them. The same principle applies in keeping your mind free from corruption and contamination. The Bible says:

Let the words of my mouth, and the meditation of my heart, be acceptable in thy sight, O LORD, my strength, and my redeemer (Psalm 19:14).

A lot of truths are stored in the Scripture. The most prominent is that the meditation of a person's heart may be either acceptable or unacceptable to God. This makes us to understand the facts that there are acceptable and unacceptable meditations. The meditations of your heart are acceptable unto God when it conforms with divine expectation. They are unacceptable when they are contrary to the word of God.

Being a sharp shooter and a prayer addict, the psalmist, who wrote these words under the inspiration of the Holy Spirit, knew the importance of the frame of mind in relation to receiving answers to prayers. If you fail to take care of the condition of your heart you will end up with ineffectual prayers.

A brother once entertained evil thoughts but was exposed by God. He was a Sunday school teacher and was very effective in church activities. This made many members of the church to think of him as one of the best Christians around. He was well favoured by the pastor and his wife. In fact, the pastor's wife constantly showered him with monetary and material gifts. She always bought something for him during her many overseas trips. While all these went on, nobody knew that the brother was battling with serious defilement of the heart as well as unimaginable secret sins.

The cat was however let out of the bag when the pastor ran into the brother, one day, as he was smoking a stick of cigarette. As soon as the brother sighted the pastor, he quickly threw the burning stick of cigarette into his pocket, not knowing that the pastor had spotted him from afar off on his bicycle. When the pastor got to him he stopped his bicycle, got down and engaged the brother in a long conversation. The cigarette fire kept burning in the brother's pocket but he tried not to do anything about it. Until it burned to his skin.

At this point, the brother's discomfort could no longer be kept from the pastor as he constantly scratched his thigh. The pastor, who knew what was happening, deliberately kept the conversation going until the cigarette burnt its way out of the brother's pocket and fell on the ground. As the brother looked at the cigarette on the ground open-mouthedly, the pastor shook his head and went away sorrowfully. This was how the sin which the brother had been struggling to conceal was blown open.

A little boy came across a creature that looked like a small dog in a bush behind his parents' house. The animal, which looked like a special brand of Alsatian dog, fascinated the boy. Because the animal looked so small, innocent and harmless, he took it and hid it in the attic of their house without telling his parents. Whenever he was given food, he would share it into two equal halves and take one portion to the animal in the attic.

As the parents noticed that the boy developed the habit of climbing into the attic they asked him what he always went up there to do. Neither the boy nor his parents knew that he was nursing a young lion inside the house. The boy and the young lion remained the best of friends for as long as he kept taking food to it in the attic. However, a great tragedy befell the family when the boy forgot to feed the lion for one whole week.

The day he remembered, he quickly carried some food and rushed into the attic. He met the lion lying weakly on the attic floor and before he could place the food on the floor the lion sprang up and descended on him. Thus the young lion made its owner its first human meal. By the time the boy's yells and moanings brought his parents into the attic, all they met remaining of their son were pieces of his flesh and bones.

The boy's case was a typical example of inviting destruction into one's life. Other people have invited evil into their lives through the sins they kept secret.

CATEGORIES OF DELIVERANCE CANDIDATES

Those who enrol for deliverance are generally divided into three categories:

- Those who find the enemy in their lives by inheritance.

- Those who invite the enemy into their lives by personal decision.

- Those who unconsciously invite the enemy into their lives.

The third category is the most difficult group to deal with. These days, many people are consciously busy inviting the enemy to their lives. But the danger becomes heightened when you are not aware of the problem. When the mind is not kept free from evil influence, it will eventually land you in big trouble, regardless of your spiritual stamina.

When you win a man's mind you have captured his thoughts, and when you capture a man's thoughts he will come under your control.. That is why satan fights tooth and nail for the control of the minds of men and women. The Bible says:

But I fear, lest by any means, as the serpent beguiled Eve through his subtilty, so your minds should be corrupted from the simplicity that is in Christ (2 Corinthians 11:3).

Satan corrupts, influences and manipulates the minds of people, including Christians. The ease with which he achieves his goal is simply amazing.

For example, why are many Christians finding it difficult to memorize the Scriptures? The answer is simple: the devil is busy removing the word of God from their hearts. The devil also turns people's minds into theatres of his operation by making their minds wander during prayer.

The extent to which the devil influences your thought is the extent to which he can control your actions. The moment human beings no longer hand their minds over to the devil he will be thrown out of business as most of what he does in the lives of people generally start from their minds.

Satan has instant access to the minds of men and women immediately their minds wander during prayer. Most bodily afflictions start from the mind. This means that if you lose the battle in the realm of the mind, you will lose the whole battle. If you win the battle in the realm of the mind then, you have won the battle. It becomes your responsibility, therefore, to barricade your mind against all kinds of satanic interference.

The devil has a complete picture of all your thoughts and imaginations and has the ability also to discern whether a motive is pure or impure. In other words, nothing is hidden from the devil. The fact that he knows our strengths and weaknesses means that he knows the best way to attack us and succeed. He has the power to make people forget good things and remember bad things. No matter how good your ideas may be, he can, through ignorance or carelessness on your part, remove them from your mind.

He has a superb knowledge of what goes on, on earth, more than we ourselves know. He keeps a data bank of all our faults, mistakes and strengths and knows just which one to use against us as the occasion arises, be it in the form of suggestions or prodding or outright commands. Because of his masterly control of people's minds he is able to make them forget to do what will make them to please God. That is why the Bible says, "There is a way that seemeth right unto man but the end thereof are the ways of death."

A sister once came to me with a funny prayer request. She said, "Man of God, just pray for me. I want to marry a pilot. I don't want to marry any other person except a pilot". I said to her, "Why don't you allow the Lord to choose for you? Don't choose a husband based on his profession". But the sister was so obsessed with her desire for a pilot as husband that the devil manipulated her into getting outside God's will.

Of course, the devil provided a pilot husband for her but the pilot showed his true colours by beating her up during their period of courtship. The devil so gained total control of the sister's mind by making her to go ahead to marry the pilot that had turned her into a punching bag even in their courtship days.

The devil usually designs evil and clever suggestions and matches them with our weak points. Even when we hesitate, he prods us on by telling us that what he is telling us to do is for our own good. He is an expert in the art of deception and counterfeit fabrication. The best way out of his ploy is to cast one's lot with the Lord. Hardly can anyone succeed at beating him by playing his evil game.

Who is really in control of your mind? Can you truly say that the Holy Spirit has fully taken charge of your mind? If your mind is under the influence and control of the spirit of God, how then would you explain the presence of evil materials in your hand? The devil's power of suggestion is so terrible that even Jesus Christ was made to sweat in the garden of Gethsemane before He could resist it.

The devil made Him to reconsider His stand concerning the cup of suffering. Jesus prayed: "Father, make this cup to pass over me". But thank God, that He made up His mind to drink from the cup. He said, "Not my will but thy will be done."

Most battle grounds generally have two forces. The mind however differs as a battle ground in that it has three forces fighting there: God, the devil and the flesh. The combination of these forces in the mind of man makes it a delicate place. It is such a small place yet big enough for so many things to be hidden there from fellow human beings. But nothing is hidden from God and he cannot be deceived. While man looks at the outward appearance He looks at the heart and sees everything going on there.

Your outward appearance may be captivating and dazzling but God will have nothing to do with you if your mind is in an objectionable state. It is possible to impress the pastor with your three-piece suit or your expensive traditional attire but God is hardly impressed by any of these things. For example, if it were possible to impress God with outward appearances, He would not have reckoned with a man like Elijah who did not wash his clothes for three years. Yet Elijah was one of God's favourite prophets.

Evil and ungodly thoughts can be likened to opening the door of your heart for satanic garbage to be thrown into it. Until your heart is brought under divine control, you cannot experience a wholesome mind. You must get to a stage in your life where your heart is lifted up to a height where it is in total conformity with the will of Christ. Such a height may not be easy to attain but you owe yourself the duty of striving to get there. When you do, you have won an important battle. There, it becomes easy for you to receive your miracles and breakthroughs. But if you are still at that level where the enemy occupies your mind completely and feeds you with the bread of sorrow, you are a non-starter in the realm of spiritual growth.

If the devil can keep you depressed for a whole day, then he is the one controlling your life. This situation will hinder you to know what it means to exercise victory and dominion over the devil.

Most of the people who come to church today are living on the fringe of divine blessings where most of what they receive can be classified as just an overflow of the blessings of God. They do not receive the real thing. They do not know what it means to receive the real showers of God's blessings, all they receive are trickles. Why? They engage in a self-deception while they think they are deceiving God by harboring evil thoughts in their minds. And as long as they possess this unwholesome mind, the Lord would hold His divine blessings back from them.

The deliverance of your mind will usher great changes into your life. There are many wonderful experiences which you will never know until you allow God to renew your mind. The moment your mind receives from the Almighty God a touch of transformation, you will begin to experience superlative blessings. Your experience will then agree with the Scriptures:

"He gave me beauty for ashes and the oil of joy for mourning and the garment of praise for the spirit of heaviness that he may be glorified".

To understand the meaning of receiving beauty for ashes you need to understand what ashes were used for. It was customary in the past for those who were bereaved or sorrowful to sprinkle ashes upon themselves. Those whose minds were free from evil domination generally experienced the putting off of the garment of sorrow and putting on the garment of praise. Paul and Silas were surrounded by sorrow and had every reason to resign to it, but when they heard the voice of God telling them to go to Macedonia, they obeyed.

Something happened when they got to Philippi. They had an encounter with a very wealthy woman who was a seller of purple clothes. Purple clothes were used by extremely wealthy people in those days. The wealthy woman got converted and decided to invite the men of God into her home. They were treated to an executive reception. For both Paul and Silas, it was a major breakthrough in the spreading of the gospel. However, there was a turn of events the following day when Paul and Silas cast out a demon from a young girl. It was then they were attacked and dragged to the marketplace. At the end, they found themselves in prison. By the time they were locked up in the prison, there were multiple wounds and bruises on their bodies. I am sure you can imagine what it means to be dragged on the ground for a long time. Whoever has gone through such an experience would never forget the excruciating pains that went with it.

In the days of Paul and Silas, criminals were beaten with both cane and sharp objects. Any person taken through such experience would end up with seriously mutilated flesh.

The physical environment in which Paul and Silas found themselves left no room for anything but sorrow and sadness. The prison in which they were kept was so dark that it was natural for them to feel gloom and despair.

Surprisingly, today, many people who find themselves in situations far happier than Paul and Silas' often become moody and despondent. I wonder what such people would do if they should find themselves in a harsh and hostile environment.

What Paul and Silas went through was enough to make them complain bitterly but there was never any negative response from them. Although their bodies were hurting, their minds were controlled by the Holy Spirit. An average modern Christian would have broken down in tears. Others would go into an ominous silence.

The first thing we notice about Paul and Silas is that they were able to pray. A lot of modern day believers readily lose their power of prayer when confronted with a little problem or trying situation. Paul and Silas did not only pray, they also sang praises to God. The totality of their action and reaction showed that they were able to exercise control over their circumstances.

When you allow what is going on around you to dictate the condition of your heart, you will allow depression and discouragement into your heart. If you allow depression to fill your heart, you will miss the miracle that you are supposed to receive.

For Paul and Silas to have been able to sing praises to God that midnight, they must have been in high spirits. The midnight hour is the darkest hour for most people. Paul and Silas prayed and sang praises to the Lord until the prisoners heard them. A lot of Christians are not able to praise God whenever faced with a negative situation, not to talk of raising up their voices to attract the attention of those around them.

Depression has made a lot of people to lose great blessings in life. If you allow the enemy to capture your mind and make you become depressed, you will lose great victories. One minute of depression can take you 20 years away from your miracle. The foundation of the prison would not have shaken and doors would not have opened if the minds of Paul and Silas were not in tunes with God. The prisoners would not have been set free and the jailer would not have been saved if Paul and Silas had resorted to weeping or crying.

Are you putting on the garment of praise where you are now or are you overwhelmed by the spirit of heaviness? What is your response to the suggestions which the devil tries to put into your mind? What is your reaction to the general economic situation in your country? Is your heart filled with faith or are you eating the bread of sorrow? Are you dancing to the tune of the devil? Are you playing the role which the devil wants you to play? Are you playing into the hands of the devil through what you allow into your mind? Are you behaving as if all the problems in the world were stacked against you?

The Bible says, "For as he thinketh in his heart so is he." Your thoughts denote the kind of person you are. The issue of the heart is so serious. The Scriptures reveal that God destroyed mankind in the time of Noah, on account of the wrong state of man's heart:

And God saw that the wickedness of man was great in the earth and that every imagination of the thoughts of his heart was only evil continually (Genesis 6:5).

God sent judgment to man because He knew that all the evil things which man did originated from his heart. Similarly, if God were to open the heart of everyone who goes to church today, a lot of people would become so embarrassed that they would never go to church again.

Another instance of divine judgment in the Scripture can be found in the 11th chapter of the book of Genesis:

And the LORD said, Behold, the people is one, and they have all one language, and this they begin to do: and now nothing will be restrained from them, which they have imagined to do. Go to, let us go down, and there confound their language, that they may not understand one another's speech. So the LORD scattered them abroad from thence upon the face of all the earth: and they left off to build the city.

Therefore is the name of it called Babel, because the LORD did there confound the language of all the earth: and from thence did the LORD scatter them abroad upon the face of all the earth (Genesis 11:6-9).

God scattered the people because of the imagination of their hearts.

You need to examine your heart today. What kind of thoughts do you entertain? Do you entertain evil thoughts in your heart while you go about speaking in tongues?

The importance of taking care of the mind is stated in Proverbs 4:23:
Keep thy heart with all diligence for out of it are the issues of life.

If you want to avoid being trapped by your tongue, you must watch the issues that come out of your mind, since what you speak is determined by the state of your heart. To be wholesome in the realm of speech, you must start working on your mind. Conscious efforts must be made and serious warfare prayer must be carried out if you want to live a life completely free from bondage. If you allow God to thoroughly work on your mind, you will begin to speak the right words at all times. If you take care of everything else without taking care of the state of your mind, you will continue to live in bondage. The moment your mind receives healing and deliverance, you will experience a turn-around in every area of your life.

PRAYER POINTS

1. Father, in the name of Jesus, I invite the ministry of deliverance into my mind, in the name of Jesus.

2. You powers of darkness, release your hold upon my mind, in the name of Jesus.

3. I rebuke all the spirits operating against the soundness of my mind, in the name of Jesus.

4. I release my mind from every bondage, in the name of Jesus.

7 The Backslider in Heart

I would like you to read this chapter very carefully. We all want revival, we all want the Lord to move. Many of us are clamouring for the supernatural. We have read the history of the church and we have heard about the move of the Lord in the past and want Him to move like that in our day. But then the revival must start in us before it becomes a global or general thing.

In every situation where there was a revival, one thing happened first of all: Repentance. This means that all backsliders must return home for fire to fall.

Without clearing off the backsliding spirit there can be no revival. And I maintain that if we of the present generation are not very careful we may not see any revival, at least of the kind we read in books. That word 'revival' has lost its real meaning.

When there is real revival, it will be impossible for men and Women to walk in the street and utter godless words, this is because, if they do, the judgement of God will fall upon them on the spot.

When there is revival, sinners would be so afraid and would revere the Lord. They will tremble in the spirit and cry. When there is revival, there will be no need for special meetings and sensational advertisements. Every shop will become a pulpit and somebody would be sharing the gospel in every working place, and every heart will become an altar.

When there is revival, every home will become a sanctuary of prayer and people will be rushing to find God. This kind of revival being talked about is not a form of entertainment neither does it come as a result of any advertisement. It is God-sent and people will attend.

This makes it different from our modern-day evangelistic revival or campaigns, where there could be large crowds, and hundreds or thousands of people get born again but with little impact on the community. But in a true revival coming from God, the spirit of God, like a cleansing flame, will sweep through the stronghold of the devil and he will begin to tremble and those who have once closed their door to Jesus will throw it open to Him and run back to Jesus.

This is what we mean by true revival. Those who do not want to know will know, those who do not want to hear will hear; everybody will know that something is happening because it is impossible for holy fire to fall upon a place and fail to attract attention, just like the apostles heard a sound of a mighty, rushing wind, and saw holy film show. Men and women gathered there and began to talk about God and on the spot, three thousand people got born again. At the next one, five thousand people got born again, and on and on like that. These men had no microphone, they did not have television sets, nor were there radio adverts. I pray that God will bring down true revival.

For those who are members of the Mountain of Fire and Miracles Ministries, the Bible type of revival is the type we pray to see in our church. If backsliding is in your heart, you are one of those delaying the revival. In Jeremiah 3:22, we read this exhortation:
Return, ye backsliding children, and I will heal your backsliding.

Likewise, in Hebrews 6:1-3, we read:
THEREFORE leaving the principles of the doctrine of Christ, let us go on unto perfection; not laying again the foundation of repentance from dead works, and of faith toward God, of the doctrine of baptism, and of laying on of hands, and of resurrection of the dead, and of eternal judgement. And this will we do, if God permit.

All these things which apostle Paul listed above are primary school items, which mean that anyone who has not gone beyond these things is certainly not growing. Verse 4-6 reads:
For it is impossible for those who were once enlightened, and have tasted of the heavenly gift, and were made partakers of the Holy Ghost, and have tasted the good word of God, and the powers of the world to come, if they shall fall away, to renew them again unto repentance; seeing they crucify to themselves the Son of God afresh, and put him to an open shame.

The Lord has sent me to warn through this book, and this message you are reading is from the heart of God. You have to take a decision after reading the book to make a covenant with the Lord. Backsliding is a terrible thing, and in the above Scripture we see its result.

In the same book of Hebrews 10:38-39, we read:
Now the just shall live by faith: but if any man draw back, my soul shall have no pleasure in him. But we are not of them who draw back unto perdition; but of them that believe to the saving of the soul.

Again, II Peter 2:20-22 tells us:
For if after they have escaped the pollution of the world through the knowledge of the Lord and Saviour Jesus Christ, they are again entangled therein, and overcome, the latter end is worse with them than the beginning. For it had been better for them not to have known the way of righteousness, than, after they have known it, to turn from the holy commandment delivered unto them. But it is happened unto them according to the true proverb, The dog is turned to his own vomit again; and the sow that was washed to her wallowing in the mire.

What terrible words we have there. And if we go back a little bit to the book of Galatians 2:18, we shall find:
For if I build again the things which I destroyed, I make myself a transgressor.

The above verse means that, those things which the Lord has helped you pull down in your life, if you build them up again, you make yourself a transgressor. Likewise, if we go to the book of Matthew 12:43, we shall hear Jesus talking to us:
When the unclean spirit is gone out of a man, he walketh through dry places, seeking rest, and finding none.

What is the implication of the above verse? It means that when you undergo deliverance, all the evil spirits depart from you, but do not go too far. They still roam around, observing you to see whether you will go back to what you were doing which will again open the door for them into your life.

Verse 44-45 says:
Then he saith, I will return into my house from whence I came out; and when he is come, he findeth it empty, swept, and garnished. Then goeth he, and taketh with himself seven other spirits more wicked than himself, and they enter in and dwell there: and the last state of that man is worse than the first. Even so shall it be also unto this wicked generation.

Perhaps you have engaged in juju and fetish things before getting born again. Don't be deceived, the spirits are still very much around the corner. Perhaps you were a fornicator before, or a proud person, or you were delivered from familiar spirits, water spirits, spirit husband, these have not moved too far from you. Perhaps you were drinking and smoking before, those spirits are still around. Perhaps you were moving about with assorted women. They are still very much around and are watching you so that at anytime that you open any door, they will once again move in and take possession of your life.

The Lord has asked me to warn you through this book that if you should go back to those things from which you have been delivered, the end will be far worse than the beginning for you. In this present dispensation, if anybody fails to live a holy life and makes a mistake, the devil will ensure that he kills him on time, before he has time to repent again.

Many people come to church with all manners of evil spirits from which they were delivered. Should they fail to keep that deliverance the enemy will pull them out and burden them with far weightier problems than they had been delivered from.

Some who have not been patient enough for Jesus to deliver them from their troubles have gone ahead to use the "wisdom of the servant" which has turned out to be their undoing.

Backsliding is a terrible thing. The word 'backslide' means to turn away from God. The Scriptures pay so much attention to it because it is something that hurts the heart of God. Of course, when a person puts Jesus Christ on the cross and crucifies Him again, God is justified in feeling disappointed.

Backsliding is turning back from the gospel to satan. Once you have turned back to the devil, with the aim of using God as a mere powerful fetish material, you have backslided. This is why the Bible has taken so much time to explain and to give many descriptions of backsliding. I shall give you some of these descriptions:

- ✓ Trying to serve two masters (Matthew 6:24).
- ✓ Forsaking the Lord.
- ✓ Going your own way (same as above).
- ✓ Leaving our first love.

- ✓ Forgetting God.
- ✓ Falling away.
- ✓ Turning aside like a deceitful bow.
- ✓ Growing cold (Matthew 24:12).
- ✓ Departing from the faith.
- ✓ Putting your hand on the plough and looking back.
- ✓ Salt that has lost its flavour.
- ✓ Light that has become darkness.
- ✓ A dog returning to its vomit.
- ✓ Crucifying the Son of God afresh.
- ✓ A dead branch.
- ✓ A disease.

A child may be excused for running away from a wicked home. But when a child leaves a tender loving mother and an affectionate father and runs into the forest, what shall we say of that? If the sheep quits an empty field for a greener pasture, who shall blame it? But when the sheep leaves a green pasture and forsakes the still waters, and goes bleating in the forest among wolves, playing in the midst of danger, one should conclude that the sheep is either mad, bewitched or foolish. In the same way, when a man leaves a caring father- our Father in heaven- and goes back to the devil, that man is either foolish, bewitched or mad. This is what happens when a person backslides.

A backslider does not wake up one morning and go out to commit adultery. Backsliding happens over a period of time during which the backslider becomes slack in his thought life, when he starts to entertain fleshy desires. From the corner of his eyes, he must have been watching nude pictures of men and women.

King David watched Bathsheba undressing. He was there when the woman wanted to start having her bath. David should simply have made a round about turn and returned into his palace, but he stayed there watching the woman undress, having her bath and, soon, he landed in trouble. A backslider is a man or woman who is operating below divine expectation. The Lord expects you to be an idol breaker in your family, but if the idol is breaking your own head instead, you are a backslider. When the Lord expects you to deliver your people but instead they succeed in pulling you back to go and serve their own idol, you are a backslider.

Spiritual decay is a gradual process. It is just like the onslaught of many diseases. The disease comes silently, and gradually wastes away the sufferer. This is exactly what happens in the heart of the backslider. Little by little, backsliding sets in. As a result of this, he watches what he should not be watching; he begins to say what he should not say; the books he should not read, he begins to read them; what he should not behold, he starts beholding and admiring and all these may be nearly unnoticed until they become a deep-seated disease in his life.

It may begin with a general feeling of indifference by which he becomes slack in his church attendance and in his Bible reading. As he tends to lose his focus on spiritual things, the flesh comes up and begins to seek fulfilment, and the same fellow who used to do three days dry fast and would look as if he had just started, would wake up early in the morning and feel very badly like eating something. He rushes to the kitchen at night and if there is no food there, he would soak garri and drink.

With time, his prayer life begins to get squashed among other interests like T.V. viewing, video, sports, parties, vagabond friends with whom he would engage in endless talks. By the time these friends leave him, he is too tired to do anything and he sleeps. With time, his spiritual power ebbs. And as his heart is filled with junk food, his hunger for the word of God diminishes.

Although he may thirst for the word of God, hardly will he be able to read it and with time, he begins to blame his church for its laxity in imparting the word of God and begins to attend that church only occasionally. If he is a Sunday school teacher, he would only come when people who admire him would be around. After some time, his fear of God departs and the priorities in his life would be re-ordered. His spiritual life begins to receive the least attention.

At this point he may begin to have the overall feeling of being lost, and spiritual discontentment comes in. He may then carry his Bible to go and attend a special seminar somewhere, whereas the simplest thing that God has asked him to do - repentance - receives no attention from him. All his activities would be geared towards shutting this out of his mind. Most wealthy men have T. V. sets in every room in their house, including the toilet. The devil uses this to distract their attention and keep them from hearing what God is telling them. Then one day, the fellow will now notice that the hatred for sin is gone. At this juncture, the devil calls a party to which demons are invited to come and rejoice.

The backslider would begin to justify his own action as his heart steadily begins to turn into stone and the voice of God becomes distant. What worries me most is that the Bible talks about some people who perpetually backslide. This class of people may be present there in the church, but their minds would be far away in Kaduna or London. Such people may be able to stay on track for some weeks, but then they are off the track. God does not want such people.

While backsliding is not something that sets in suddenly, it may escalate rapidly once it sets in. You cannot ascend the mountain of the Lord when you put your vehicle in the neutral gear. That little sleep, slumber, folding of the hands, that little leaven leavens the whole lump. The little foxes are the ones that spoil the vine. Those little sins, those little confusions that the enemy is able to introduce soon begin to cause big problems. The Bible is the word of God which remains true all the time.

A very brilliant student may not be tempted by the devil to cheat in an examination because he knows very well that his brain is very sharp. But when the devil wants to bring him down, he would make him to be very proud. Satan is an unfair tempter. Even after a 40-day dry fast, he still went to the Lord Jesus Christ to hit Him below the belt by asking him to command stones to turn into bread.

A Christian might not be tempted to commit murder or steal money in the office, but can be made to gossip and backbite, through this, backsliding comes. Therefore, beloved, backsliding is primarily a thing of the heart and is often concealed. There are many backsliders in the Bible. The Bible makes this very clear to us, and that is why it is such a source of worry to genuine believers everywhere. That which has to go from our lives must go so that we can become what God wants us to be.

Solomon was a backslider; David backslided; Saul and Asa backslided. Asa had a sore in his leg but never went to God. He went to meet his juju men and got into trouble. Jonah was a backslider. The children of Israel backslided so many times. Peter was a backslider and so was Thomas. If you open your Bible, you will read about a fellow called Demas who was a backslider too. Think about this as you read this message. Where do you stand? Is God waiting for you at point 10 while you are at point 6?

Something within you is crying out for something better, crying out for a higher fire. Something within you is telling you that you are not on your destined mountain, and asking you to move fast, but you are not moving. That is backsliding. It does not matter if you have been attending church service for many years, you may even be a foundation member and yet remain a backslider. It does not matter from which church you have come to M. F. M., you may have carried over your backsliding from your former church and still continue to backslide. You have to examine yourself; examine your heart and tell the Lord to search your heart. If there is any unclean thing there, it must be cleansed out.

God is not a respecter of persons, but in every generation, whoever loves Him and keeps His commandments is accepted of Him. The Lord is forever present with you, so talk to Him now. If you want a revival in your life, it is better to hold nothing back from the Lord. There is danger in being a backslider in the heart. The enemies of Israel laughed Israel to scorn when Israel backslides.

If you have ever read Psalm 137, you must have noticed that it is a lamentation of backsliders by the rivers of Babylon. But it was already late, for what was to happen had already happened.

WHAT CAUSES BACKSLIDING?

The cause can be hidden or open.

- **Bad relationship**

  If you really want to make heaven, avoid all those unfriendly friends lest they succeed in pulling you into their own camps. Any friend who feels uncomfortable whenever you talk about Jesus is not the kind of friend who should be visiting you regularly. Any friend whose interests run contrary to yours is certainly not the kind of friend you should be seen with. The Bible says that evil communications corrupt good manners.

This is why it is spiritual abomination for you to say that you are born again and suddenly say you want to marry an unbeliever. This means you are planning to backslide. It means you are not interested in making heaven because that partner will ensure that he or she shakes anything that concerns heaven away from your hand. He or she may be following you to church now only to make you backslide when you are properly caged-in. All the bad friends will make you backslide. Avoiding the fellowship of God's children, sexual immorality and such other vices will bring backsliding.

- **Spiritual poverty**
  When you listen to heresy and inadequate teaching of the word of God, and you exhibit poor foundation, spiritual blindness, deliberate disobedience to the Lord, and you neglect your prayer life, all these will result in backsliding. The Bible says that if we wilfully sin after we have acquired the knowledge of the truth, there remaineth no longer any sacrifice for sin but a certain fearful judgment.

And if you escape from the pollution of the world and go back into these entanglements, the Bible says it would have been better if you had not known about salvation. Unbelieving is part of spiritual poverty. Neglect of prayer life is also part of it. And they all cause backsliding.

- **The love of the world or compromise causes backsliding**

8 Spiritual Circumcision

We shall start off this chapter by reading from the book of Deuteronomy 10:16-17:

Circumcise therefore the foreskin of your heart, and be no more stiff-necked. For the LORD your God is God of gods, and Lord of lords a great God, a mighty, and a terrible, which regardeth not persons, nor taketh reward.

A similar verse is in the book of Jeremiah 4:4:

Circumcise yourselves to the LORD, and take away the foreskins of your heart, ye men of Judah and inhabitants of Jerusalem: lest my fury come forth like fire, and burn that none can quench it, because of the evil of your doings.

Again, in the New Testament, in the Acts of the Apostles 7:51-54, the children of Israel were addressed in the same manner:

Ye stiff-necked and uncircumcised in heart and ears, ye do always resist the Holy Ghost: as your fathers did, so do ye. Which of the prophets have not your fathers persecuted? And they have slain them which shewed before of the coming of the Just One; of whom ye have been now the betrayers and murderers: who have received the law by the disposition of angels, and have not kept it. When they heard these things, they were cut to the heart, and they gnashed on him with their teeth.

And when we go also into the book of Romans 2:28-29, we read:

For he is not a Jew, which is one outwardly; neither is that circumcision, which is outward in the flesh: but he is a Jew, which is one inwardly; and circumcision is that of the heart, in the spirit, and not in the letter; whose praise is not of men, but of God.

God started the principle of circumcision with Abraham and then ordered all male children in Israel to be circumcised. What is circumcision? Circumcision is the removal of the foreskin in a male child. And what is that foreskin? It is that place of insensitive skin covering the male organ at birth; circumcision takes place when this skin is removed.

In the olden days, when spies were caught in Israel, the first thing done to them was to undress them and when they were found to be uncircumcised they were instantly put to death, for that was a sign that such people were not Jews.

The blunt truth, beloved, is that God is more interested in what is going on inside you, than the outward thing. God does not look the way man look. A man may look at your face and conclude that you are a man of God, or a holy person, but God who sees the heart knows who you are. He is more interested in what is going on inside.

All those outward confessions or professions of Christianity do not matter to God as does what goes on inside your heart. That is why Paul said in the above verse that this circumcision of the outside is far from being the real thing, and that the only thing that matters to God is the circumcision of your heart. This means that the spiritual foreskin covering the heart should be cut off.

When we talk of anything creating a barrier between God and us, the major one is the flesh. The flesh is the major opposition to what God wants to do in our lives. And for God to insist that all male children in Israel should be circumcised, and that they could not relate to Him until they were circumcised, meant this was a very serious affair.

Abraham was circumcised at the age of 99. So, the real Christian is the one circumcised in the heart by the spirit of the living God.

You can sing without being circumcised in the heart; you can preach without being circumcised in the heart, you can do all manners of things without being circumcised in the heart but, one day, something will happen: the trumpet will sound and there will be a division - those that are circumcised in their hearts, God will take them away from here; and those that are still hiding behind the foreskin in their hearts shall remain here. And the way things are going on now, the end may be closer than we think.

The time has come for all of us to be very serious. Each time we take our Bible we need to read it seriously, when we witness we need to witness seriously and when we pray, we need to pray seriously because we never can tell what the end-time will meet in our hands. That is why the Bible says, "Whatsoever your hand findeth to do, do it heartily as to the Lord," because we don't know when the end will come or what it will meet in our hands. This means that wherever we don't wish the time to meet us we should never go there at all, because the Bible says, "The day will come as a thief in the night" without warning. And let us always remember that, the Bible says that as it was in the days of Noah and Lot, and their people were enjoying themselves and couldn't care what they were saying, so are many preachers laughed at and mocked today.

It took Noah 120 years to build the boat, and one day, after he had completed it, he began running after animals - lizards, fowls, birds, crocodiles etc, and watching their sexes as he did so. I am sure that, at that stage, many people would have looked at him and shaken their heads in pity at the sight of a man they must have taken for insane, because they did not know what was happening. The Lord told Noah not to put the window of the ship at its side but on top.

Why did God say this? It was because God did not want him to have demonic mercy on those human beings, because if he had the window at the side, and the flood started, a lot of them would cry for Noah's help. With the position of the window, the only place Noah could look at was the heaven. The same thing is about to happen now. Many people are still coming to church with uncircumcised hearts. The Bible says that the heart of man is desperately wicked and asked, "Who can know it?" It will take God's circumcision to deal with our hearts. When a male person is not circumcised there is a collection of materials inside the foreskin which can cause some problems. It is the same thing when we have uncircumcised hearts. Though we may look and sound like Christians, we shall remain impure before the Lord. This is because no matter how well an uncircumcised man may dress, he remains but a destruction looking for somewhere to happen.

A person may be able to perform all functions in the house of God yet his heart may not be circumcised. The uncircumcised in heart are difficult to identify, and as long as a person's heart remains uncircumcised he is just like death roaming about. In all those traditions where circumcision is practised, an uncircumcised child cannot easily undress among his colleagues; he would be ashamed to be different from the others.

It is the same situation with the uncircumcised in the heart. They hide themselves under a lot of covers - over-spirituality, over-goodness to others, etc. They hide a lot of things from their pastors, their friends and their prayer partners.

A 72-year-old man was embarrassed the day he came to see me to pray for him. Immediately he sat down he talked about all the problems he had gone through – how they took his wife and children away together with everything he had. When he finished, I asked him to let us pray together. During the prayer, I found this old man naked in the presence of another woman equally naked. I stopped the prayer and I asked him his age and he said 72 years. I asked him when last he slept with a strange woman who was not his wife, and he said that very morning. I there and then asked him to go out, kneel down in the open and ask God for forgiveness. The woman he slept with was a bean cake seller he had met somewhere around. The man was a typical prayer collector or one of those we call time wasters.

Circumcision of the heart takes a painful procedure. The uncircumcised in the heart have things in their lives which, when exposed, cause them pains. And because of the pains they are sure to experience, they hide their state of uncircumcision.

Nobody can circumcise himself. Every believer that comes in through the door must surrender himself to God to be circumcised. If you don't allow this, God has nothing to do with you and in this lies a lot of dangers.

In the Bible, circumcision was a covenant between God and man. For you to have a deep and clean relationship with God, you must submit your heart to His circumcision. Moses was almost killed by God because his son was not circumcised. So uncircumcision in us can lead to a lot of trouble.

As you read this, I want you to check your heart. Is your heart right with God? Have you removed the foreskin of your heart? Many oppressions will stop if we can circumcise our hearts. A lot of deliverance prayers shall become unnecessary if we could circumcise our hearts. When the men of war were about to fight in the Scripture, they asked the uncircumcised not to come along. Circumcision of the heart then is the need of the hour. Without it, God will put you aside and use someone else because an uncircumcised heart cannot fulfill His agenda.

When our hearts are not circumcised, it means we are stiff-necked. To be stiff-necked is to reach the terminal stage of disobedience. For this, we need to check our hearts. If our hearts are still evil, we are uncircumcised. But if our hearts are clean, we are circumcised. If your heart is still desperately wicked, then you are uncircumcised. If your heart is weak, it means it is yet to be circumcised; but if it is thick in God, no matter your situation, it has been circumcised.

If your heart is deceitful, it is uncircumcised; but if it is faithful, it is circumcised. So you need to check now what is happening inside your heart.

If your heart is ever wavering, it is not circumcised; but if it is honest, it is circumcised. If your heart is hard and rebellious, it is uncircumcised; but if it is true and contrite, it is circumcised. If your heart is proud, it is uncircumcised; but if it is humble and tender, it is circumcised. If your heart is foolish, it is a sure sign that it is not circumcised.

God looks at the heart. A man may be looking at your face, but as far as the Bible is concerned, God looks at the heart. God spoke to Samuel: "Look not at the eye of this man, for I have rejected him." God does not look the way man looks. It may be hard for man to differentiate who is who among people coming to church, but as long as your heart is not right with the Lord, you are deceiving yourself. You need to do something quick.

In the house of God, it is difficult to differentiate between those who come with satanic agenda and those who come to worship God in truth; but one day the truth shall be revealed, and God will find a replacement. God wants a change of heart. He wants us to pray to Him and ask Him to circumcise our hearts, so that we would be free to serve Him.

When you are circumcised in the heart you have reached a point of no return where you will burn the bridge behind you.

You need to close your eyes and look back at your recent past. Check the thoughts that crossed your mind during the period. Were they the thoughts of heaven? Were they the thoughts of purity? Was there any time you allowed your heart to wander away from the Lord? If, for example, as you are reading this now, the Lord says, "Son, it is okay, come, your work has finished,"as you go up to Him, will He smile and say, "Well done!" Or do you know in your heart that you are working behind schedule, that all you have been seeing in the dream that God wants you to do, you have not even started doing them?

Of course, you are not getting younger; so you need to check your heart. Jesus may come at anytime. Are you pursuing His agenda for your life, or you are busy procrastinating in that vision you know that He wants you to actualise? You need to ask for the blood of Jesus to bring quality repentance into your heart so that each time you pray, the promise of the word of God will come to pass, and the Lord will hear as you yet speak with your mouth.

Anything that would hinder you from receiving instant answers to your prayer, you need to pray for the blood of Jesus to wash it away. You need to pray to the Lord with the heart of the blind Bartimaeus, the man who cried out to the Lord Jesus Christ, and Christ could not help but listen to him. Bartimaeus' cry put a brake on the Lord from that moment on. When a cry puts a brake on the Almighty, the Almighty refuses to go forward until He listens to the crier and acts on his petition. Whenever this happens, it signifies a breakthrough. The Bible says: "It is the day that I cry then shall my enemies turn back. This I know for God is with me."

PRAYER POINT

1. O Lord, lay your hand on me and say unto me, "Fear not," in the name of Jesus.

2. Let every fear depart, in the name of Jesus.

3. O Lord, circumcise my heart by your spirit, in the name of Jesus.

4. (Lay your hand on your head) O Lord, kill every satanic deposit in my life, in the name of Jesus.

5. Every pursuing dragon, die, in the name of Jesus.

6. It is written: the God of peace shall bruise Satan under my feet. O Lord, fulfil this promise in my life, in the name of Jesus.

7. (Lay your hand on your head) The enemy will not remove my star, in the name of Jesus.

8. The Lord liveth, blessed be my rock, my enemies will not have their way, in the name of Jesus.

9. Awake! Put on your strength, O Zion, and fight for me, in the name of Jesus.

10. Every pipeline of failure in my life, be destroyed, in the name of Jesus.

11. Every seed of failure in my destiny, be roasted, in the name of Jesus.

12. Every power insisting on my destruction, I withdraw your peace by fire, in the name of Jesus.

13. O God, arise and let me be singled out for breakthrough, in the name of Jesus.

14. In the mighty name of Jesus Christ, I will make it.

15. O God, arise and let people bless me everywhere I go, in the name of Jesus.

16. O Lord, let people compete to do me good, in the name of Jesus.

17. My negative dreams will not come to pass in my life, in the name of Jesus.

18. I shall not die but live and declare the name of God, but my Goliath shall die, in the name of Jesus.

19. O God, arise and let my enemies rise against one another, in the name of Jesus.

9 Prayer Warfare

POWER AGAINST THE SPIRIT OF CONFUSION

1. I pull down the stronghold of the spirit of confusion in my life, in the name of Jesus.
2. Every city of confusion within my mind, be broken down now, in the name of Jesus.
3. Let the storm of confusion within my mind be still, in the name of Jesus.
4. Every cloud that has enveloped my mind, fade away now, in the name of Jesus.
5. I reject any form of confusion, I claim sound mind, in the name of Jesus.

POWER AGAINST THE SPIRIT OF MIND DESTRUCTION

1. Any power that wants to destroy my life, I command you to be destroyed, in the name of Jesus.

2. Every faulty foundation in my life, I command you to receive the fire of God, in the name of Jesus.
3. I send back to the sender, every evil arrow of mind destruction fired against my life, in the name of Jesus.
4. My mind, receive the touch of God and be renewed, in the name of Jesus.
5. Lord, strengthen my inner mind with your fire and your power.

DELIVERANCE FROM UNCONTROLLABLE THOUGHTS

1. I pull down every stronghold of uncontrollable thoughts in my life, in the name of Jesus.
2. I cast down every evil imagination in my heart, in the mighty name of Jesus.
3. I bring into captivity every area of my thought life to the obedience of Jesus.
4. In the name of Jesus, I break the power of evil remote controllers over my thought process.
5. I fill up every doorway of evil uncontrollable thought with the blood of Jesus.

CASTING DOWN IMAGINATIONS

1. I scatter to pieces every evil imagination against me, in the name of Jesus.
2. I command all imaginations contrary to my prayer life to be defeated, in the name of Jesus.
3. I cast out and bring to nought every demonic imagination against my family, in the name of Jesus.
4. I immunize my spirit, soul and body against every vain imagination, in the name of Jesus.
5. I cast down, I plunder, and I frustrate, every satanic imagination against my life, in the name of Jesus.

PULLING DOWN STRONGHOLDS OF IMAGINATION

1. Lord, I pull down every stronghold of the enemy over my life.
2. I pull down and roast every demonic ladder the enemy uses to enter my life, in the name of Jesus.
3. I come against evil pronouncement against my life, in the name of Jesus.

4. I arrest and bind every satanic notebook opened for my life, in the name of Jesus.
5. I cancel every evil imagination of the enemy upon my life, in the name of Jesus.
6. Blood of Jesus, cleanse my heart of every evil thought in the name of Jesus.
7. My heart, be delivered from every evil thought, in the name of Jesus.
8. I free my heart, from every evil thought, by the fire of the Holy Ghost, in the name of Jesus.
8. Heavenly thought, fill my heart now, in the name of Jesus.

AUTHORITY AGAINST MIND CONTROLLING FORCES

1. You my mind, in the name of Jesus, you will not push me to hell, in the name of Jesus.
2. You habitation of darkness inside my mind, be desolate, in the name of Jesus.
3. Every evil attack on my mind, be defeated, in the name of Jesus.

4. You my mind, receive the touch of fire, in the name of Jesus
5. In the name of Jesus, I will make it in life.
6. Sting of death, release my mind, in the name of Jesus.
7. Sting of fear and failure, release my mind, in the name of Jesus.
8. I command all heavy burden in my life to roll away and burn to ashes, in the name of Jesus.
9. Blood of Jesus, replenish my heart.

PARALYSING THE STRONGMAN WORKING AGAINST THE MIND

1. You power corrupting my desire and my mind, be roasted in the name of Jesus.
2. You strongman of evil imagination paralysing good things in my life, be paralysed, in the name of Jesus.
3. Lord, revive my mind with your fire, in the name of Jesus.
4. Lord, put your law into my mind, in the name of Jesus.

5. All the good things that the strongman of the mind has paralysed, receive life and be restored to my life, in the name of Jesus.

LOCATING HIDDEN TREES IN THE MIND

1. I locate every hidden evil tree in my mind with the fire of God, in the name of Jesus.
2. I uproot every evil hidden tree in my mind, in the name of Jesus.
3. You evil fruit, die, in the name of Jesus.
4. You planters of evil trees in my life, be roasted, in the name of Jesus.
5. O Lord, begin to plant good things into my life and let them manifest in my life, in the name of Jesus.

POWER AGAINST EVERY SPIRIT OF UNCERTAINTY

1. I bind and cast out the spirit of uncertainty in my mind and I destabilize its control over my life, in the name of Jesus.

2. Holy Ghost, occupy every area that the spirit of uncertainty has in my mind, in the name of Jesus.
3. Father Lord, every damage that the spirit of uncertainty has done to my life, repair and restore it, in the name of Jesus.
4. I cast out every spirit of uncertainty in every area of my life, in the mighty name of Jesus.
5. I recover every good thing that I lost to the spirit of uncertainty, in the name of Jesus.

SPIRIT OF MIND BLINDNESS

1. Holy Spirit, possess my mind, in the name of Jesus.
2. You spirit of mind blindness, loose your hold over my life, in the name of Jesus.
3. I renounce you spirit of mind blindness in my life, in the name of Jesus.
4. I regain my words, I regain my values, I regain my spiritual gift that I lost to the devil through the spirit of mind blindness, in the name of Jesus.

SPIRIT OF DEATH AND HELL

1. Throughout the days of my life, the gate of hell will not prevail over me, in the name of Jesus.
2. You power of hell, release all my belongings that are under your control, in the name of Jesus.
3. As for me and my household, our names shall not enter the book of hell, in the name of Jesus.
4. You spirit of death, you will not prosper in my life, in the name of Jesus.
5. I release the life of Christ into my life, in the name of Jesus.

SPIRIT OF MIND WASTAGE

1. My mind, I command you to think aright, in the name of Jesus.
2. All mind controlling spirits, be bound, in the name of Jesus.
3. You producer of evil thoughts, somersault and die, in the name of Jesus.
4. Holy Spirit, renew my mind to glorify God in the name of Jesus.

5. Father Lord, soak my mind with heavenly revelations, in the name of Jesus.

DELIVERANCE FROM FRAGMENTED MIND OR CONSCIENCE

1. I gather together every area of my mind that is scattered in the name of Jesus.
2. Every area of my life and mind in satanic cage, be released in the name of Jesus.
3. I plead the blood of Jesus into my mind and the whole of my life, in the name of Jesus.
4. I fire back every arrow of the enemy fired into my mind, in the name of Jesus.
5. I command you, my mind: go back to your resting place, in the name of Jesus.

THIS BOOK AND MORE ARE OBTAINABLE AT:

*** MFM Press Bookstore**

54, Akeju Street, Off Shipeolu Street, Onipanu, Lagos. **Contact:** 01-814-4074

*** MFM International Bookshop**

13, Olasimbo Street, Onike, Yaba.

*** The Battle Cry Christian Ministries**

322, Herbert Macaulay Way, Sabo, Yaba, Lagos.

*** IPFY Music Konnections Limited**

48, Opebi Road, Salvation Bus Stop

Contact: 234-1-4719471, 234-8033056093

*** All MFM Church branches nationwide and Christian bookstores.**

About the Book

Keep thy heart with all diligence; for out of it are the issues of life. **(Pro. 4:23)**

There are physical and spiritual sicknesses that plague men day and night. Many minds are sick. This book is targeted at bringing deliverance to the mind.

Do you find that your mind is uncontrollably filled and manipulated by lust, anger, rejection, evil fantasies, confusion, torment, oppression, dejection, frustration, pollution etc.

Grab a copy of this book and your life will no longer remain the same.

About the Author and MFM

Dr. D. K. Olukoya is the General Overseer of the Mountain of Fire and Miracles Ministries and the Battle Cry Christian Ministries. The Mountain of Fire and Miracles Ministries' Headquarters in Lagos; Nigeria is the largest single Christian congregation in Africa, with attendance of over 100,000 in single meetings.

Dr. Olukoya holds a first class honours degree in Microbiology from the University of Lagos, Nigeria and a PhD in Molecular Genetics from the University of Reading, United Kingdom. As a researcher, he has over seventy scientific publications to his credit.

Anointed by God, Dr. Olukoya is a prophet, evangelist, teacher and preacher of the Word. His life and that of his wife, Shade, are living proofs that all power belongs to God.

ISBN 978 - 36917 - 6 - 7

Printed in Great Britain
by Amazon

25957559R00106